Indian Music in Education

This book has two aims: to act as a ~~r~~ ... North Indian classical music for teachers in schools, and for others working in music education; and to show how Indian music may be introduced in a creative and fruitful way into today's music classroom.

This is a practical book: a special feature is the sequence of assignments for pupils, which is designed to help develop in them the sense of structure crucial to understanding Indian music. The assignments are supported by a cassette, with examples played on *sitār* and *tablā*.

About the author

Gerry Farrell studied music at Dartington College of Arts and at Goldsmiths' College, University of London. He then went on to further research and study in India, much of which was funded by grants and scholarships from the Dartington Hall Trust and the Indian Council for Cultural Relations. He is now based in London, and is well known for his performances on the *sitār* and the guitar, some of which are with the contemporary music group, Shiva Nova. His work in music education includes planning and teaching music courses on Indian music throughout the London area. He has had a number of articles on Indian music and education published in the British press.

RESOURCES OF MUSIC HANDBOOKS

Indian Music
in Education

RESOURCES OF MUSIC HANDBOOKS

General Editor: John Paynter

RESOURCES OF MUSIC HANDBOOKS

INDIAN MUSIC IN EDUCATION

GERRY FARRELL

The right of the
University of Cambridge
to print and sell
all manner of books
was granted by
Henry VIII in 1534.
The University has printed
and published continuously
since 1584.

CAMBRIDGE UNIVERSITY PRESS

Cambridge

New York   Port Chester   Melbourne   Sydney

Published by the Press Syndicate of the University of Cambridge
The Pitt Building, Trumpington Street, Cambridge CB2 1RP
40 West 20th Street, New York, NY 10011, USA
10 Stamford Road, Oakleigh, Melbourne 3166, Australia

First published 1990

Printed in Great Britain at the University Press, Cambridge

British Library cataloguing in publication data
Farrell, Gerry
   Indian music in education – (Resources of music handbooks)
   1. Indian music
   I. Title   II. Series
   781.690954

ISBN 0 521 36771 9

QO indicates item on the accompanying cassette ISBN 0 521 38411 7, available
separately through your bookshop or, in cases of difficulty, direct from the
Educational Sales Department, Cambridge University Press.

Design: Claire Brodmann
Photographs: David Runnacles
Cover illustration: by kind permission of the India Office Library,
Foreign and Commonwealth Office
Cover design: Paul Oldman

PN

Contents

For my parents, and for Jane

Introduction

This book is about a problem of musical translation – about how the classical traditions of North Indian music may be taught, enjoyed and appreciated within the context of Western music education.

North Indian classical music has a complex and highly evolved system of teaching. This methodology has developed over the centuries and is embodied in the *guru-shishya parampara,* the master–disciple tradition. This is a close and intense relationship, operating on a one-to-one basis with the pupil spending extended periods of time with the teacher and perhaps even living in the teacher's home like a member of the family. Most of the musical information is imparted by word of mouth (although the use of tape-recorders is changing the meaning of this), or by writing with the system of notation known as *sargam.* As important as the pupil's own lessons is the process of sitting in on more advanced students' tuition, and listening to the teacher practise or perform – in other words, soaking up the ambience of the musical life that surrounds the *guru.* The most crucial element in this way of learning is time; although working within strict formal parameters, the heart of Indian music lies in improvisation, and this must be absorbed in a very different fashion from written music.

How can such a system be transferred into Western music education? On the face of it this would seem to be an impossible proposition – there is no existing framework within our system of music teaching to accommodate it, and anyway such a method of teaching could not operate in the same manner outside the appropriate cultural environment. However, Indian music is now enjoyed by the concert-going public in the West, and is also a vital cultural force within our own Asian communities. Recent multi-cultural education policies have stressed the need for teaching Indian music, and world musics in general, as an integral part of the music curriculum.

Yet teachers, being unfamiliar with the theory and practice of Indian music, may find it difficult to use in a creative and fruitful way in the course of their work. The purpose of this book, therefore, is twofold:

1 To function as a resource on North Indian classical music for teachers and others working in the field of music education.
2 To show how Indian music may be introduced in teaching and creative music-making through a sequence of assignments that develop the sense of structure that is crucial to understanding Indian music.

This book focuses specifically on the classical music of North India for several reasons:

1. North Indian classical music is the Indian music system most familiar in the West.
2. Other forms of Indian music (e.g. Hindi film music) borrow heavily from classical music in terms of melody, rhythm and instrumentation. So classical music is useful as a starting-point as it embodies techniques and materials that can be re-worked later.
3. North Indian classical music provides a clear and unique model of how to improvise with melodic and rhythmic material.
4. The South Indian system differs substantially from the Northern in form and instrumentation. Although it is of great interest, South Indian music deserves separate detailed treatment, and so will not come within the scope of this book. Also, all the information in this book stems from personal experiences as both a student and teacher of North Indian music; any discussion of South Indian music would be purely theoretical in this respect.

The term 'North Indian classical music' is used here as elsewhere: as a generic musical term. It encompasses music and musicians from Pakistan and Bangladesh as well as from India.

This book should not be seen as some sort of 'short cut' to understanding and teaching Indian music. Like any other music, Indian music can only be properly understood and used in teaching when a knowledge of its background has been gained and the basics firmly grasped. The book was structured with this in mind.

Part 1 introduces Indian music in terms of its geographical, historical and aesthetic contexts. The various genres of Indian music are also described here: vocal, instrumental, religious, popular, and so on.

Part 2 introduces the melodic and rhythmic structure-principles of North Indian classical music – *rāg* (melody) and *tāl* (rhythm) – and describes how these elements connect in a performance. This is approached through assignments and exercises using *rāg* and *tāl*, and by demonstrating their function in the wider context of Indian music performance practice.

Part 3 looks at improvisation in Indian music, and how this may be developed into the process of composition.

Part 4 is about North Indian instruments: their names, methods of tuning and general maintenance. Also, which instruments are most suited to particular age groups in schools.

Inevitably this book makes use of Indian musical terminology. I have tried to avoid using convenient translated equivalents such as *rāg* = mode. Such translations are not only misleading but they also imply a continual process of reducing all music to a Western standard. Such comparisons, and staff notation, are only used where they seem essential to understanding the musical concept under discussion. Much of the structure of Indian music will, at first, seem strange and new, but it becomes familiar more quickly when Western preconceptions about music structure are dropped and the music is accepted on its own terms. Then the unique form and beauty of the music shine through, and Indian music becomes yet another exciting dimension to the teaching and enjoyment of music.

Note on transliteration

There is great variance in the manner in which Indian musical terminology is transliterated.

I have consulted many sources to check spellings and pronunciation, but my principle sources have been *A Practical Hindi–English Dictionary,* ed. M. Chaturvedi and Dr B. Nath Tiwari (Delhi, 1984) and *Outline of Hindi Grammar,* R. S. McGregor (Oxford, 1972).

Here are a few examples of how the vowels in some of the more commonly used terms are pronounced:

rāg, tāl, thāt:	the 'a' sounds like the 'a' in 'bath'
gat:	the 'a' sounds like 'u' in 'gut'
tīntāl:	the 'i' sounds like 'ee' in 'teen'
sitār:	the 'i' sounds like 'i' in 'sit'.

I have indicated plurals by adding 's' at the end of the word.

Acknowledgements

Author's acknowledgements

Many people have helped me in my studies of Indian music and the writing of this book.

Firstly I would like to thank my teachers of the *sitār* and Indian music: Ahmed Egan, Alistair Dick, Suresh Mishra, Amarnath Mishra and Professor Debu Chaudhuri. Many fellow musicians have helped me to understand various facets of Indian music; the complex art of *tablā* playing: Yousuf Ali Khan, Lewis Riley, Nick Wiltshire, Vijay Kangutkar, Jaspal Bhogal; the *sarod*: Swami Anand Tosho; vocal music: Aziz Zeria.

Special thanks are due to my brother Desmond who first introduced me to Indian music, and Di Mitchell who encouraged me to take it up as a serious study. Colleagues and friends in various fields have helped and encouraged me over the years with my studies of Indian music and culture through their questions, advice and criticisms: Mike Vaughan, Max Paddison, Natalie Webber, John Baily, Robert Plowright, Jim Fall, John Goff, my brother John, and many more too numerous to mention here.

Thanks also to John Paynter, Annie Cave and Peter Nickol for their help and advice at all stages in the preparation of this book.

Other acknowledgements

Author and publisher would like to thank Minal Shah, Alpa Vaghela and Mr Jaspal Bhogal, who appear in the photographs; and Mr S. D. Gupta (Indian Music Promotions, Southall, London), who kindly loaned the Indian musical instruments, photographed.

PART ONE

The background to Indian music

The background to Indian music

India is a vast country which encompasses a diverse and complex array of languages, customs, religions, terrains and climatic conditions. The music of India is similarly multi-faceted. India is rich in classical, folk, popular and religious musical traditions, each with a unique range of identities and forms. Some of these musics have origins that stretch back thousands of years; others are products of the twentieth century. Indian music, in its many forms, is in a state of continual development and change.

The classical music of North India as we know it today is the outcome of a long process of synthesis and adaptation brought about by the various Islamic invasions of the North from the ninth and tenth centuries onwards. The invaders brought with them their own musical systems and instruments, and over a long period of time these merged with existing Indian musical forms. This epoch in North India's history also accounts, to a large extent, for the differences between the North and South Indian systems. Music flourished under the patronage of the Mogul emperors in the sixteenth, seventeenth and eighteenth centuries, and it was during this time that many of the classical musical forms were developed and refined. This was also the era of the great musical theorists, performers and composers like the legendary Tansen (*circa* 1506–89). Stories of Tansen's musical powers have since taken on mythical proportions: allegedly he could start fires, melt stones and mesmerise listeners with his singing. These colourful stories echo some of the similarly fabulous tales that surround the musical prowess of various Western composers and performers.

Tansen is said to have had tremendous occult power and to have performed miracles through his music. By singing *Raga Deepak*, he was supposed to have been able to light the oil lamps, or by singing *Raga Megh Malhar*, to bring rain. Tansen was said to be *nad-siddha*, which means he had complete mastery over sound, especially musical sound.

Ravi Shankar, *My music, my life*

There also evolved an intricate aesthetic dimension to Indian music. *Rāgs* were said to embody the essence of a particular mood, and should be played only at certain times of the day or seasons in the year. Each *rāg* was considered to be either male or female (male – *rāg*, female – *rāginī*), and was designated as belonging to a particular family of *rāgs*, usually relating to specific scale types. This imbuing of musical forms with human characteristics was visually represented in *rāg-mālā* paintings, exquisite allegorical miniatures depicting the aesthetic meaning and spirit of the *rāg*.

As the courts of India declined under British rule, the position of musicians also changed (the British were not patrons of Indian music, nor indeed of any Indian art forms). Deprived of the patronage of the courts, music became a profession centred upon the large urban areas such as Delhi and Calcutta. Indian classical music became a city music because that was where the work was to be found, and the new patrons were the urban middle classes. The musicians belonged to *gharānās* (literally, households). These guild-like organisations developed particular stylistic identities, and musical information was not passed readily between them. Rather, there was rivalry, and fierce loyalty; particular compositions, ways of singing, etc. were guarded jealously. Although members of *gharānās* did not need to be members of the main teacher's family, this was often the case, and it was assumed that such members received the best tuition and were given special musical material. Although *gharānās* are no longer a vital or potent musical force in the contemporary reality of North Indian classical music, musicians will still say with pride that they belong to this or that *gharānā* and, perhaps, that their lineage stretches back to the great Tansen himself. Nowadays the *gharānā* is chiefly a symbol of tradition and continuity.

In the twentieth century, music and other traditional art forms became important symbols in the struggle for independence from Britain. And since independence in 1947 Indian classical music has become one of the major expressions of Indian culture abroad, personifying continuity of tradition yet carrying all the excitement of a music improvised and recreated anew at each performance.

Although present-day Indian classical music is the heir to older traditions, in many respects it would be unrecognisable to a musician from the Mogul courts. The foremost vocal style of those times, *Dhrupad*, is rarely heard now, having been supplanted by *Khyāl*, a florid and less austere form of singing. Also the *sitār* has become the most popular stringed instrument along with the *sarod*, taking over from older instruments such as the *bīn*.

Rāg and *tāl,* however, continue as the basic structural ordering principles of the music, and these will be discussed in detail in this book. Because of the resilience of *rāg*, with its seemingly endless potential for variation, Indian classical music has remained melody-based. Western harmonic ideas have made few significant inroads into Indian music. Although the British were concerned with imposing a particular social order on Indian society, music did not play a major part in this. The small portable harmonium used by missionaries was absorbed into traditional Indian music, but its function was re-defined to suit. It has now become a common accompanying instrument in classical music, but the four-part harmony of the Christian hymns has not carried over. Where Western influence is most apparent is in Indian pop music, but even here harmony is not used in the same way, and the modality common to other genres of Indian music still predominates. Indeed, this ability to adapt, absorb and re-define musical elements from other cultures is a hallmark of Indian music. Despite the hybrid mix of guitars, cellos, drums, basses, *sitārs, tablās, dholaks,* and many other instruments found in Indian film music, the result is always, somehow, quintessentially Indian. Much of the reason for this lies in the power of the unique structural principles of Indian music: linear melody over cyclical rhythm. These principles have been honed to perfection in the practice of classical music.

A typical North Indian classical music ensemble, whether vocal or instrumental, consists of three basic musical elements:

1   A soloist singing or playing the melody
2   A percussion instrument, either *tablā* or *pakhāwaj*
3   A drone instrument, either harmonium or *tānpūrā*

Indian music is small-scale, like Western chamber music. Although there have been experiments in Indian music using larger ensembles akin to Western orchestras, this cannot be considered a common feature of classical music performances. However, duets involving two soloists, known as *jugalbandi* (literally, to tie a pair), have become increasingly popular in recent years.

A recital usually follows a stylised sequence of musical events which will be described in detail in Parts 2 and 3 of this book. Because the music is largely (though not totally) improvised, the length of a piece is not pre-determined. The exposition of a *rāg* can take anything from a few minutes to several hours depending on how the musician feels. All-night concerts are popular in North India, and it is at these events that the most detailed versions of *rāgs* can often be heard.

The performances of Indian classical music that we hear in the West, either live or on record, are mostly of a much shorter duration. This does not mean that the music has been watered down or changed;

9

such is the flexibility of Indian musical structures that the essence of a complex *rāg* can easily be rendered on one side of an album. Indeed in the hands of such players as the great master of *sitār* Vilayat Khan, the crux of a *rāg* can be played in a few phrases.

I have already mentioned improvisation. This skill lies at the heart of Indian music. What is of particular interest within the context of this book is the way in which Indian music offers a fascinating model of how to improvise with melodic and rhythmic material in a structured manner. The expertise of an Indian musician is measured by his or her ability to improvise fluently and intelligently while keeping within the parameters and grammar of the *rāg* and *tāl*. Indian audiences are in general extremely knowledgeable about the details of various *rāgs*, and will show their approval by exclamations and affirming gestures of the hand when some particularly subtle or exciting phrase is played. This response from the audience is an important and integral part of any Indian concert. When the musicians first started performing on radio, many found the absence of audience communication so disturbing that they were unable to sing or play properly. However, All India Radio (AIR) has since become a major source of employment for musicians, and in true Indian style they have adapted their performances of *rāgs* to suit the tight time schedules and unresponsive studio atmosphere.

Next let us look in more detail at the different types and styles of Indian music.

The generic term for music in India is *sangīt*. This term has always had a wider meaning than how we understand the word 'music' in the West. *Sangīt* encompasses music, dance and drama. These three elements were always linked in Indian culture, even though nowadays distinctions are generally made between recitals of music, dance and other performing arts.

Indian classical music falls into two broad categories: vocal and instrumental. However, they should not be thought of as entirely separate musical entities. The voice is considered to be the ultimate medium for musical expression, and instruments relatively limited, but all instruments and instrumental techniques have a close affinity with vocal music. The *sitār* is designed so that the strings can be pulled laterally to produce the smooth flow between notes common in vocal music; on the *tablā* each stroke is known as a *bol* (word), and a series of syllabic sounds are taught for each composition. A *tablā* player can recite whole compositions with the voice, giving them a lilting rhythmic sense of phrasing. There are many other examples of this overlap between voice and instrument in Indian music; the voice is the source from which all music flows.

10

Vocal music

Two vocal forms have already been mentioned: *Dhrupad* and *Khyāl*. Performances of *Dhrupad* are now rare although it was once the foremost genre of vocal music. The name of this kind of vocal music derives from the Sanskrit word *druvapada*: *druva* – structured or fixed, and *pada* – word or syllable. This indicates the importance of text or lyrics in the performance of *Dhrupad,* but this and other forms of Indian classical vocal music should not be thought of as songs. The words occupy a very small part of the performance – most of it consists of abstract vocalising either with meaningless vocal sounds or using the names of the notes in *sargam,* i.e. *Sa, Re, Ga* (see Part 2 for details). Traditionally *Dhrupad* was always sung by men. It is usually accompanied by one or more *tānpūrās* (drone instruments) and a double-headed, barrel-shaped drum called the *pakhāwaj.* Formerly *Dhrupad* was also accompanied by the plucked stringed instrument the *bīn* which would follow and elaborate the vocal line, but in performances of *Dhrupad* now this is rarely the case. On the occasions when the *bīn* is now heard in a recital it is usually played as a solo instrument. (In fact there are very few players of this instrument still performing in North India.)

In contrast to *Dhrupad, Khyāl* is very popular and is performed extensively throughout India. *Khyāl* is an Urdu word which can be translated as 'thought' or 'imagination'. Again *Khyāl* came to fruition in the Mogul courts, and although its origins are unclear it was thought originally to have been a synthesis of *Dhrupad* and *Qawwalī,* a type of Muslim religious song. Whatever the origins of *Khyāl* it was soon established as the foremost style in North Indian classical vocal music.

Khyāl and *Dhrupad* differ in many respects as regards performance practice and musical detail. The most immediately apparent contrast is in the types of ensembles. *Khyāl* is sung by both men and women, and the accompanying instruments are the *tablā, sārangī* and/or harmonium, and *tānpūrā.* Both *sārangī* and harmonium fulfil the function of supporting the voice melodically. This is achieved by 'shadowing' the vocal line, i.e. playing the same line as the singer a fraction of a second afterwards. The singer will be improvising, so one can appreciate the level of aural perception required by the *sārangī* or harmonium player. Formerly it was only the *sārangī* that played this role. This is a bowed instrument which uses heavy gut strings. It is notoriously difficult to play, mainly because the notes are stopped by sliding the back of the fingertip, on the cuticle, along the string. The American ethnomusicologist Daniel Neuman gives a vivid account of his own learning process on the *sārangī,* and how he found it difficult in the initial stages to learn 'the beauty of mutilated

11

cuticles . . .' (Neuman, 1980: 32). Not surprisingly the harmonium has nowadays virtually taken over the *sārangī*'s role in *Khyāl*; but the harmonium can never match the mellifluous vocal quality of the *sārangī*, which is as close as any Indian instrument gets to the voice with its endless subtleties of inflection. Solo instrumental recitals on *sārangī* are now more common.

A performance of *Khyāl* falls into several definite sections: a slow composition known as *baṛā* (large) and a faster composition known as *chotā* (small). These compositions can be set to various *tāls* but a common format is: slow – *ektāl* (12 beats), and fast – *tīntāl* (16 beats) (see Part 3 for details). What is particularly striking about a performance of *Khyāl* is the various ways in which the voice is used. The lyrics of *Khyāl* are usually on romantic or religious themes, but the words of the *chīz* (composition) do not play an important part in the performance in a literal manner, and when the words have been sung, usually only once in their complete form (the *chīz* is usually in two sections known as the *sthai* and *antera*, similar to A and B sections in a Western song), they give way to abstract vocalising either using the syllables of various words from the text, or what is known as *ākār* (using the sound 'ah'), or with *sargam*. The main phrase of the *chīz*, called the *mukhṛā*, is used to bring improvised sections to an end, usually on the first beat of the *tāl* which functions as a cadence point. The *mukhṛā* is the only part of the lyrics which is continually returned to throughout the performance.

Another common form in North Indian vocal music is *Ṭhumṛi*. This is usually sung by women, and although similar in sound to *Khyāl* is generally considered a 'lighter' classical genre. *Ṭhumṛis* are more akin to songs. They are based on particular *rāgs,* but these are not explored in the detailed and extensive manner typical of *Dhrupad* and *Khyāl*. However, the lyrics in *Ṭhumṛi* have relatively greater importance. *Ṭhumṛi* is typically accompanied by harmonium, *tānpūrā* and *tablā*.

Other vocal forms that should be mentioned are *Qawwalī* and *Bhajan*. Both of these are religious song-forms, Muslim and Hindu respectively. Although not considered classical music as such, many aspects of their performance resemble the vocal genres already outlined, especially in instrumentation and vocal delivery. Another popular form is the *Ghazal*. This is a light classical song form usually on the theme of love, using an Urdu text. It is very popular in North India and particularly in Pakistan. The melodies of *Ghazals, Qawwalīs* and *Bhajans* may also be based on various *rāgs*.

This is a brief outline of various vocal forms current in North Indian music. Of course there are others not mentioned here; an exhaustive description would easily be the subject of an entire book. For example, the rich folk music tradition has not been mentioned at all. As in all musical cultures, the streams of folk, popular, and classical – often arbitrary terms anyway – mingle and influence each other, but for the purposes of the present book classical music provides the best model of how the unique structural elements of Indian music operate.

The central importance of the voice in Indian music cannot be emphasised too strongly. As we shall see in more detail later, much of Indian musical terminology, whether applied to vocal or instrumental music, derives from a vocal perspective. Indian instruments may appear complex and unapproachable, but in order to take part in Indian music, all anyone has to do is open the mouth and sing (but that, of course, may not be too easy either!).

Instrumental music

In the twentieth century, instrumental music has become increasingly popular in North India. Again this is a trend that has its roots in the Moghul courts, though the supremacy then of vocal music was never in question. Nowadays instrumental music is at least as widely listened to as vocal music, and in many ways is even more popular. Instrumentalists like Ravi Shankar, Vilayat Khan, Ali Akbar Khan and Amjad Ali Khan have the status of superstars in India, and often enjoy a similar fame abroad. A concert featuring any of these artists is sure to be a sell-out in India. Few vocalists command that sort of following except perhaps in the pop music scene.

There are many instruments played in Indian classical music, but the most commonly heard are the *sitār* or *sarod* as solo instruments, and the *tablā*, harmonium and *tānpūrā* as accompanying instruments (though it should be noted here that the last two play a very different role from the *tablā*, as we shall see later). The *sārangī*, *esrāj* and *dilrubā* are bowed solo instruments. Rarer plucked stringed instruments are the *surbahār* (like a bass version of the *sitār*) and the *bīn* (already mentioned in connection with *Dhrupad*). The main wind instruments are the *shehnai*, a double reed instrument similar to the shawm or oboe, and the *bansurī*, a bamboo side-blown flute which, although primarily a folk-instrument with limited range, has been adapted for use in classical music.

Although the solo instrument may vary, there is a typical stylised format for a performance of instrumental music. The influence of vocal music is reflected in many aspects of instrumental performance but there are also other elements which derive purely from the nature of the various instruments and the musical possibilities they offer. Although instrumentalists seek to emulate the flow and subtlety of vocal music, they never

13

merely copy it. (The influence appears to be two-way, with vocalists introducing instrumental-like sounds into their performances – but this is a controversial and contentious subject amongst musicians, and vocalists often deny the instrumental connection.)

An instrumental performance usually includes the following sections: *ālāp, jor, gats* and *jhāllā.* The structure of these sections will be explored in detail in Parts 2 and 3, but briefly they can be described as follows:

> *Ālāp* – unaccompanied, non-rhythmic exploration of the *rāg*
> *Jor* – unaccompanied, with regular pulse
> *Gats* – compositions with improvisations set to *tāl,* with *tablā* accompaniment
> *Jhāllā* – fast rhythmic climax with *tablā*

(Please note that 'unaccompanied' here means without *tablā.* Drone instruments would be present throughout *ālāp* and *jor.*)

A particular feature of instrumental recitals is the complex interplay that takes place between the *tablā* and the solo instrument. Although the primary function of the *tablā* is accompaniment, it does not merely keep *tāl* but also interacts with the solo instrument, responding to the flow of the improvisation and taking solo breaks. The best performances of instrumental music are more akin to duets than 'soloist/ accompanist'. Sections of *jawāb-sawāl* (question-answer), in which intricate phrases are swapped between soloist and *tablā* with ever-increasing speed and rhythmic complexity, are great favourites with audiences. (It has to be said that in the wrong hands *jawāb-sawāl* can degenerate into a crass display of showmanship – but also that such displays are much liked both in India and the West!)

Generally speaking there is less variation of performance practices in instrumental music than in vocal music. Although the differing styles of, for example, Ravi Shankar and Vilayat Khan are instantly recognisable, the broad structure of their performances will still be as outlined above. It is this structure that will be presented here as a model of how to improvise with melodic and rhythmic material.

This has been a brief outline of the various styles of performance in North Indian classical music – not exhaustive, but aiming to provide the minimum background that is required to have a working knowledge of the Indian musical system. In Part 2 we will look in more detail at the way Indian music works, through *rāg* and *tāl.*

PART TWO

Rāg and tāl: the architecture of Indian music

Rāg and tāl: the architecture of Indian music

Rāg and tāl are the two structuring principles that govern Indian music. Rāg (sometimes written as raga) is the organisation of melodic material, and tāl (tala) metric.

Ways into rāg

Assignment 1

This is about how small melodic motifs are the 'identity tags' of a given rāg.

A 1 Listen to the tape, then find the notes on any instrument, or using voice:

2 Hear how the sitār player improvises with these notes.

3 Improvise with these notes, making sure they keep their melodic identity.

B 1 As before, first listen to the tape, then find the notes.

2 Again improvise with these notes, keeping their identity.

3 Now improvise with all these notes:

These are the typical melodic contours that would be heard in a performance of a *rāg* called *Yaman*. They would form the basis of the *ālāp*, the slow introductory movement of the *rāg* where the scalar relationships of the *svaras* (notes) are explored in detail.

If a musician were asked to outline the essence of *rāg Yaman* he or she would play or sing these phrases.

The most important section where the material of the *rāg* is explored is the *ālāp*. We would have to go back to the unmeasured preludes of Baroque music to find anything in Western classical music vaguely akin to Indian *ālāp*.

The *ālāp* opens the performance and introduces the listener to the character of the *rāg*, establishing the important notes and phrases and outlining the ascent/descent patterns. Typically the *ālāp* will progress from *maṅdra* to *tār saptak* (lowest to highest octaves).

In the course of the *ālāp* the notes of the *rāg* are examined in microscopic detail. Beginning from small cells of one or two notes, the musician gradually fills in the details of the *rāg* by a progressive process of *baṛhat* (growth or expansion), the tessitura eventually spanning all three *saptaks* (octaves). Great use is made of *gamaks*, the generic term for grace notes and ornamentation in Indian music (it has a very specific meaning in *sitār* playing). The subtleties of the *rāg* will also be brought out by the use of *shrutis* or microtonal alterations of the basic *svaras* (notes). Extensive use is made of *mīnd*, the smooth gliding from one note to the next. The effect of *ālāp* is flowing, without angles. *Ālāp* is slow and lingering.

Ālāp is unmeasured, but although it has no definite rhythm or pulse it does not lack direction. On the contrary, the gradual bringing into focus of all the notes of the *rāg* should be clear and well-constructed. *Ālāp* does not drift, as sometimes mis-perceived by Western musicians.

When a particular segment or phrase has been explored in *ālāp* this is sometimes indicated by a *mohṛā*, a kind of punctuation mark where the music momentarily picks up a pulse, before moving onto the next phrase when once again it is free of regular rhythm.

Because *ālāp* is extemporised it is virtually impossible to notate accurately in *sargam* (Indian notation) or staff notation. *Ālāp* is usually learnt by listening to the teacher sing or play the phrases and gradually absorbing these over a period of time. However, what notation can do is give the general outline of an *ālāp*. Filling in the detail comes with practice – as indeed is true of every aspect of Indian music.

The following example shows the shape of a typical *ālāp* in *rāg Yaman*:

Ālāp in Yaman

Sargam: D̲ N̲ N Ṁ̲ D̲ N N ᴳR ˢN ˢN D̲ N R S S, N̲ R G, G, Ṁ

G ˢN ᴳR G G Ṁ D P G Ṁ D P Ṁ G G Ṁ D P Ṁ G

R S ˢN ᴳR Ṁ G G Ṁ D N N, Ṁ D N N, D N D N Ṙ S

Apart from its purely musical purpose, *ālāp* has important practical functions for the performer of Indian music. For the vocalist it opens the voice up and accustoms it to the particular notes and tonal range of the *rāg*. For the instrumentalist it gives an opportunity to check the tuning of the instrument, let it settle down and make any adjustments necessary.

In the next assignment the music moves on, and the notes are played with a regular pulse.

Assignment 2

4 ▢ 1   Listen to how the notes are played. They still have the same identity, but now they have a regular pulse.

5 ▢ 2   Hear how the *sitār* player improvises with these notes.

6 ▢ 3   Now improvise around these notes. The tape will set the pulse to start you off. Work in two groups:

Group 1: Keep the pulse, using instruments or clapping.
Group 2: Improvise.

4   What do you think is the point of using these notes again, with a pulse?

The essence of *rāg* is that melodic material is in a continual state of change and development.

The section heard in Assignment 2 is known as *joṛ* (literally, joining), and is usually found in instrumental music, although the idea derives from a section in *Dhrupad* called *non-tom*.

As its name suggests, *joṛ* serves the function of joining the *ālāp* to the *gat* section. There is not always a distinct break between *ālāp* and *joṛ*; often one simply grows from the other. In *joṛ* the material of the *ālāp* is re-examined with a regular pulse. This is kept by strokes on the *chikāri* strings, with melodic movement on the main string:

Joṛ in Yaman

As the *joṛ* progresses the melodic density increases, and fast passages of notes called *tāns* are introduced (more on these later). Next the music takes yet another direction.

20

Assignment 3

1 Listen to the tape. The notes are the same, there's still a regular pulse, but what has changed?

2 Play the notes with these rhythmic groupings.

This further unaccompanied melodic section is known as *jhāllā*, a term which later is also used for the final (accompanied) climactic section of the performance. The unaccompanied *jhāllā* grows from *jor* and is concerned with metrical structures derived from the interplay between the *chikāri* (rhythm strings) and the main (melodic) string. It also has an equivalent in some types of vocal music.

Jhāllā in Yaman

etc.

In instrumental music this *jhāllā* marks the end of the unaccompanied part of the *rāg* (i.e. without *tablā*).

21

The *rāg* in North Indian classical music

There is no equivalent of a *rāg* in Western music. One often comes across it described as a 'scale', 'mode' or simply a 'melody'. A *rāg* contains scales (or modes) and melodies, but it is not any one of those things – it is an amalgam of these elements and much more besides. The manner in which melodic material is organised in a *rāg* is unique to Indian music; other non–Western music systems such as the Persian *dastgāh* are similar to *rāgs* but are not the same. It is not really feasible to come up with any concise definition of *rāg* in Western musical terminology without missing many essential features.

A *rāg* will have the following characteristics:

○ It will be based on a *thāt* (scale-type) which has particular intervals. A *rāg* can contain up to seven *svaras* (notes, degrees of scale), but not less than five.

○ Each *rāg* has a particular ascent/descent pattern in which some *svaras* may be omitted, or played in a particular order.

○ There will be one or two *svaras* which have special significance in the *rāg* and emerge as important focuses for melodic activity.

○ There are *pakars* (catch-phrases) which identify individual *rāgs*, and *chalans*, ways of moving melodically in the *rāg*. (See Assignment 1.)

○ Every *rāg* has fixed melodic compositions in a *tāl* (rhythmic cycle). But particular *tāls* are not assigned to particular *rāgs*.

There is also an aesthetic dimension which assigns certain *rāgs* to specific times of the days, or seasons, and also imbues them with particular moods or sentiments. This is not like programme music: a midnight *rāg* does not have to evoke the feeling of midnight (whatever that may be: midnight in London feels a lot different from midnight in Delhi!), and there might well be other reasons for linking *rāgs* with particular intervals to particular times of the day. For example, in ancient times when music and drama were closely linked, different melodies may have been used to signify the changes of time during the action, i.e. a certain melody would be played to indicate morning, evening and so on. However, there are also other more complex theories relating particular intervals to times of the day.

Indian musicians still prefer to perform *rāgs* at their associated time of day, which means that in the West we tend to hear lots of evening *rāgs*. In India there are more all-night concerts where rarer *rāgs* are heard.

Sargam

Sargam is comparable with Western sol-fa (doh, ray, me . . .). It is a system for naming notes in Indian music, and a method of notation. SA is the tonic or ground note (the note always heard in the drone that accompanies all Indian music), and the degrees of the scale are: SA, RE, GA, MA, PA, DHA, NI, SA. The names of the notes can be further abbreviated to S, R, G, M, P, D, N, S. In fact SA, RE, etc. are already abbreviated forms of longer Indian names: *Shadja, Rishabha, Gandhara, Madhyama, Panchama, Dhaivata, Nishada.* In ancient theory these names were related to different sounds from the natural world.

If all the notes are *shuddha,* i.e. 'natural', with SA represented by middle C, the scale would look like this in staff notation:

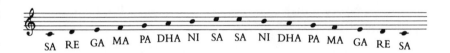

In translation to Western staff notation, C is the conventionally used pitch for SA. But like the Western 'doh', SA is movable, and the actual pitch chosen for it will depend on factors such as vocal or instrumental range.

Having determined the actual pitch of SA, SA and PA cannot then be altered relative to the 'natural' scale shown above. MA can become *tivra* (sharp), and all other notes *komal* (flat). *Komal svaras* are indicated by underlining the note-name – hence RE means RE *komal* (the flattened 2nd degree of the scale). A dash above MA indicates that it is *tivra,* thus: ́MA or ́M.

Most Indian music spans three *saptaks* or octaves: *mandra, madhya, tār* (low, middle and high respectively). Set out in staff notation it looks like this:

Notice how notes below *madhya saptak* are indicated with a dot beneath the letter name, and in *tār saptak* with a dot above.

So Indian music can be written down, but it is important to make a distinction between this kind of notation and staff notation. *Sargam* should never be thought of as a score for performing. It is a form of shorthand useful for notating compositions and other musical material, but discarded as soon as these have been memorised. *Sargam* can capture the broad outlines of musical passages, but not the melodic or rhythmic subtleties of inflection essential to the rendering of a *rāg*. *Sargam* also works as an important aid to pitch sense in the same way as sol-fa.

Thāt and rāg

Early this century the Indian musicologist V. N. Bhatkhande codified a system of ten *thāts* (scale-types) from which, he theorised, most of the *rāgs* in North Indian music could be derived. Thus the *rāgs* came first, the *thāts* afterwards.

The ten thāts

Bilaval

SRGMPDNS

Kalyān

SRGMPDNS

Khamāj

SRGMPDNS

Bhairav

SRGMPDNS

Pūrvi

SRGMPDNS

Mārvā

SRGMPDNS

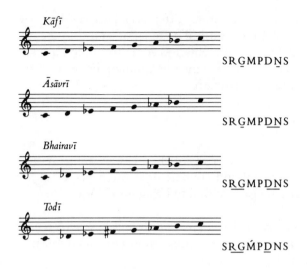

Kāfī

SRG̲MPDN̲S

Āsāvrī

SRG̲MPD̲N̲S

Bhairavī

S̲R̲G̲MPD̲N̲S

Todī

S̲R̲G̲ḾPD̲N̲S

Thāts may be seen as parent scales from which many rāgs can be derived. Several rāgs may use the notes of a particular thāt, but in very different ways. For example, from Kāfī thāt we can have rāg Kāfī, rāg Bhīmpalāsī, rāg Bāgeshrī, to name but three. The thāt represents the basic scalar material the rāg, but a thāt is not a rāg. For example, the three rāgs mentioned above exhibit important differences in their basic ascent and descent patterns:

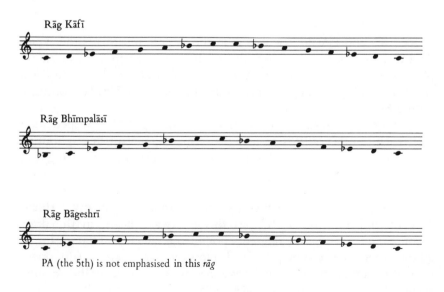

Rāg Kāfī

Rāg Bhīmpalāsī

Rāg Bāgeshrī

PA (the 5th) is not emphasised in this rāg

25

There would also be many other differences between the *rāgs*. *Thāt* is only the barest guide to the musical material of a *rāg*.

The notes we used in Assignments 1–3 come from *rāg Yaman,* a popular *rāg* in India which is often taught to beginners because of the relative simplicity of its melodic structure.

Rāg Yaman

Time and mood   Yaman is a *rāg* of the early evening. Its *rasa* (sentiment or mood) is peaceful and content. It is often played at the beginning of concerts, and is also believed to bring good luck.

Notes used   *Rāg Yaman* derives from *Kalyān thāt,* so MA is (and must always be) *tivra. Yaman* is one of the most important and frequently played *rāgs* of the *Kalyān thāt.*

Ascent and descent patterns   The *āroha/āvaroha* (ascent/descent) of *Yaman* is:

N	R	G	Ḿ	D	N	Ṙ	Ṡ	Ṡ	N	D	P	Ḿ	G	R	S

SA and PA do not appear in the ascent, and this is the typical tendency of *Yaman*. Occasionally SA and PA can appear in ascending phrases, but a performance of *Yaman* which emphasised SA and PA in ascending passages would be unsatisfactory, and would lead to confusion with other *rāgs*.

Āroha/āvaroha is a most important concept to be grasped about the structure of a *rāg*. It is an idea that remains relevant throughout the course of a performance, and is crucial in distinguishing *rāgs* coming from the same *thāt*.

Important notes   Of course an important note in any performance of Indian music is SA, as this is always heard in the drone accompaniment and is the reference point from which the relationships of all the other notes can be perceived. However, there are usually one or two other notes in the *rāg* which have special significance. In Indian music theory these are known as the *vādī* and *samvādī*. Theoretically the *vādī* is the most important note in the *rāg*, with *samvādī* of secondary importance.

In *Yaman* the important notes are GA and NI, with GA being given slightly more prominence (though some musicians consider GA and NI to be of equal importance in *Yaman*). Melodic activity will centre around these two notes. They form important structural reference points in the performance of the *rāg*. Compositions may begin or end on these notes, and improvisations will be fashioned around them.

Typical phrases　　Certain phrases in a *rāg* are like identity tags (as in Assignment 1). Typical phrases in *Yaman* are:

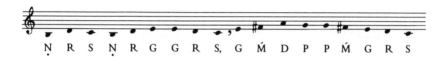

N R S N R G G R S, G Ṁ D P P Ṁ G R S

These are the typical melodic contours that would be heard in a performance of *rāg Yaman*. They would form the basis of the *ālāp*.

We have looked briefly at the first stages of a *rāg: ālāp, joṛ, jhāllā*. Next we look in more detail at the rhythmic aspect of Indian music, *tāl*.

Once upon a time Narada thought he had mastered the whole art and science of music. To curb his pride Vishnu took him to visit the abode of the Gods. In this vast building there were thousands of men and women who were all weeping and wailing over their broken limbs. Vishnu stopped and asked what was wrong. They answered that they were the *ragas* and *raginis* of music but that Narada, ignorant of the true knowledge of music and unskilful in performance, had sung them so recklessly that their features were distorted and their limbs broken. Hearing this Narada, overcome with shame and remorse, fell on his knees and begged forgiveness from Vishnu.

Ways into tāl

Tāl is a time–cycle. It is a constantly-repeating number of beats that keeps coming back round to beat 1.

Assignment 4

1   Count 16 beats, clapping on 1, 5, 9 and 13. Count the other beats quietly to yourself, or tap them with your foot. Always return to beat 1 of the next cycle of 16.

1 2 3 4	5 6 7 8	9 10 11 12	13 14 15 16	1 *etc.*
>	>	>	>	>

2   Now clap it this way:

1 2 3 4	5 6 7 8	9 10 11 12	13 14 15 16	1 *etc.*
>	>		>	>

(i.e. missing the clap on beat 9).

3   Instead of a clap, make a small hand-signal, like a wave, to mark beat 9.

4   Split into two groups. Group 1 clap on beats 1, 5, 9 and 13. Group 2 clap on 1, 5 and 13 but give the hand-signal on beat 9.

	1 2 3 4	5 6 7 8	9 10 11 12	13 14 15 16	1 *etc.*
Group 1	>	>	>	>	>
Group 2	>	>		>	>

Work together until both groups can hold their clapping patterns steady.

A *tāl* is a time–cycle: this description gives a clue to the nature of this metrical system. It is a repeating metrical unit containing a certain number of *mātrās* (beats). For example, Assignment 4 is about *tīntāl*, which has 16 beats.

Theoretically a *tāl* could have any number of *mātrās*, but the most common in Indian music are units of 16, 14, 12, 10, 8, 7 and 6.

Within the cycle, the *mātrās* will also be grouped into small units which have differing stresses or accents. These are termed *tālī* (clapped) or *khālī* (empty). A closer look at *tīntāl* demonstrates this.

Tīntāl *(16 beats)*

1 2 3 4	5 6 7 8	9 10 11 12	13 14 15 16	1 *etc.*
>Clap	>Clap		>Clap	>Clap
X	2	0	3	X

Tīntāl has four *vibhāg* or sections, each consisting of four *mātrās*. In Indian notation the signs X, 2, 3, 4 indicate *tālī vibhāg,* 0 indicates any *khālī vibhāg.* X marks the *sum* or first *mātrā* of the *tāl.* This is an important point in the *tāl* as it often marks the beginning and end of improvisations.

In *tīntāl* the four *vibhāg* begin on 1, 5, 9 and 13. 1, 5 and 13 are *tālī* and 9 is *khālī.* So when clapping *tāl,* which is the common way of keeping time in India, there would be a clap on 1, 5 and 13 with silence on 9. *Khālī* is usually marked by a wave of the hand: if clapping with the right hand onto the left palm, on beat 9 the right hand is turned palm upwards with no clap being given.

On this page and the next are some other common *tāls.* There are several interesting points to note about these *tāls:*

○ There are different ways in which the same number of beats can be grouped, as in 14 and 10.
○ There can be more than one *khālī* in a *tāl,* as in 12 and 10.
○ The *khālī* may also occur on *sum,* as in 7.
○ A *tāl* like *kaharvā* 8 is a rhythmic unit in its own right, not just half of *tīntāl* (16). Similarly *rūpak* (7) is not half of *jhūmrā* or *dhamār.*

Other *tāls*

Jhūmrā (14 beats)

1 2 3	4 5 6 7	8 9 10	11 12 13 14
>	>		>
X	2	0	3

Dhamār (14)

1 2 3 4 5	6 7	8 9 10	11 12 13 14
>	>		>
X	2	0	3

29

Ektāl (12)

1 2	3 4	5 6	7 8	9 10	11 12
>		>		>	>
X	0	2	0	3	4

Jhaptāl (10)

1 2	3 4 5	6 7	8 9 10
>	>		>
X	2	0	3

Sūltāl (10)

1 2	3 4	5 6	7 8	9 10
>		>	>	
X	0	2	3	0

Kaharvā (8)

1 2 3 4	5 6 7 8
>	
X	0

Rūpak (7)

1 2 3	4 5	6 7
	>	>
X	2	3
(0)		

Dādra (6)

1 2 3	4 5 6
>	
X	0

Every *tāl* has a particular identity. Each is a unique rhythmic unit.

Assignment 5

1 By clapping and signalling, keep each of these *tāls*: *tīntāl, kaharvā, jhaptāl, dādra, rūpak*. Practise each one until you are confident that you can hold it steady.

2 Now work in two groups, one group on 16, the other on 8.

Group 1:

1 2 3 4 5 6 7 8 9 10 11 12 13 14 15 16   1 2 3 4 5 6 7 8   9 *etc.*
>   >   >   >

Group 2 joins in with its 8-beat cycle when group 1 has completed its first 16-beat cycle.

1 2 3 4 5 6 7 8   1 *etc.*
>   >

3 The next stage is to get all the *tāls* going at the same time. Do this with five groups keeping 16, 8, 10, 6 and 7, introducing them in that order, and bringing in each new group when group 1 begins a new 16-beat cycle. The pattern becomes increasingly complex as each group enters, so take it steadily and build up in stages.

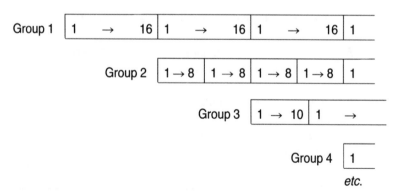

4 If you can successfully get all five groups (or even four) keeping their different *tāls* together in this way, you will be doing extremely well. To bring the exercise to a close, phase out the groups one by one. Each group should end on beat 1 of its *tāl*, and group 1, with *tīntāl*, should be the last to stop.

In the last exercise a complex pattern of cross-rhythms builds up as long as each group keeps its *tāl* intact. It may be difficult to achieve this at first, but it is worth persevering because the aural effect is exciting, especially when several groups come down on a clap together and then move off again into their different patterns. In the end everyone should be aware of the different *tāls* being kept without confusing their own particular clapping pattern with another.

One way of getting over the initial difficulty of clapping *tāls* in this way is to count out loud as well as clapping, i.e. saying every beat (1, 2, 3, 4, 5, etc.) but only clapping on 1, 5, 13, or whatever the *tāl* might be. When counting out loud, groups may become quite partisan about their own *tāl*, and consequently tend to get it right.

Assignment 6

There are ways of saying the beats in Indian music just as there are ways of saying the notes.

8 |QO| 1 Listen to the tape. The player is clapping and counting 16.

9 |QO| 2 Now 16 (*tīntāl*) is played on the *tablā* (Indian drums).

10 |QO| 3 Each beat is both played and spoken.

4 Learn to say the sounds that the player is speaking.

11 |QO| 5 Listen again. The player plays 8 (*kaharvā*) and says the sounds. This *tāl* uses a different set of sounds.

6 Learn the sounds for 8 (*kaharvā*).

7 In two groups keep 16 and 8 simultaneously, and say the sounds at the same time.

Tāl is based on additive rhythmic principles, rather than the repetition of equal divisions of beats as in much Western music. Although *tīntāl* is in equal groups of four, it should not be thought of as the equivalent of 4/4 in Western music.

One is often asked when teaching, what is the purpose of the *khālī* in *tāl*? It becomes clearer when you try to clap or play *tāl*. The *khālī* acts as a kind of signpost within the *tāl* to indicate where you are. Over a long period of *tīntāl* in slow tempo it is not feasible to count individual beats, especially if you are improvising melodically at the same time, so *khālī* is an important reference point. Although *khālī* may appear at various points in different *tāls*, it always serves this function.

Tāl in North Indian classical music

Tāl must be understood as a metric framework which defines the rhythmic dimension of the music. Within this framework numerous variations are possible, and indeed much of the skill of playing Indian music lies in the ability to manipulate the rhythm within the framework of *tāl*. The *tāl* with its basic structure always remains intact as the metric reference point but, as in *rāg*, the possibilities for variation are virtually endless.

Just as a *thāt* is not a *rāg*, so also the outlines of the *tāls* given above do not tell the whole story of how *tāl* operates. To see how *tāl* actually works we should look at the *bol* (stroke) patterns used in *tablā* playing.

A *tablā* player is manipulating several different layers of metrical information:

a   The basic outline of the *tāl*.
b   The outline realised as a *thekā* or framework of stroke patterns consisting of sets of *bols* (as in Assignment 6).
c   The distribution of these strokes across the *tālī* and *khālī* sections of the *tāl*.

Each *tāl* has a particular *thekā* or basic stroke pattern consisting of *bols*. *Bols* have a triple function:

1   To imitate the various sounds played on the *tablā* (see also Part 4).
2   As an aid for memorising compositions.
3   As a form of written notation.

Thekā

The *thekā* for *tīntāl* is:

X				2			
1	2	3	4	5	6	7	8
dhā	dhin	dhin	dhā	dhā	dhin	dhin	dhā

0				3				X
9	10	11	12	13	14	15	16	1 *etc.*
dhā	tin	tin	tā	tā	dhin	dhin	dhā	dhā *etc.*

Bols :

Each *tāl* has its own *ṭhekā*. For example:

Jhūmrā

X			2				
1	2	3	4	5	6	7	
dhin	-dhā	tirakiṭa	dhin	dhin	dhāge	tirakiṭa	

0			3				X
8	9	10	11	12	13	14	1 *etc.*
tin	-tā	tirakiṭa	dhin	dhin	dhāge	tirakiṭa	dhin *etc.*

Jhaptāl

X		2			0		3			X
1	2	3	4	5	6	7	8	9	10	1 *etc.*
dhī	nā	dhī	dhī	nā	tī	nā	dhī	dhī	nā	dhī *etc.*

Kaharvā

X				0				X
1	2	3	4	5	6	7	8	1 *etc.*
dhā	ge	nā	tī	nā	ka	dhī	nā	dhā *etc.*

Rūpak

X(0)			2		3		X(0)
1	2	3	4	5	6	7	1 *etc.*
tin	tin	nā	dhin	nā	dhin	nā	tin *etc.*

Differences between tāls

Two *tāls* which use the same groupings of beats (i.e. clapping patterns) can have different *bols*. For example, there is another *tāl* in 14 known as *Dīpchandi* which has the same beat grouping as *jhūmrā tāl* but because of the *bols* the *ṭhekā* has its own rhythmic identity:

Dīpchandi

X			2				
1	2	3	4	5	6	7	
dhā	dhin	–	dhā	dhā	tin	–	
0			3				X
8	9	10	11	12	13	14	1 *etc.*
tā	tin	–	dhā	dhā	dhin	–	dhā *etc.*

Generally speaking there is a stroke to every beat of the *tāl*, although occasionally there are rests on individual beats such as in *Dīpchandi* (not to be confused with *khālī* which refers to groups of beats).

How does the concept of *tālī* and *khālī* connect to actual performance practice?

In each *tāl*, the strokes that appear on the *khālī* differ from those in the rest of the cycle. This is something to listen for in performances of Indian music. Basically the sound of the *bāyan*, the left-hand drum, is not heard during *khālī*, and visually this is often indicated by the flat of the hand being placed on the drum head.

Further rhythmic subtleties become apparent as one listens to *ṭhekās*. Are there no strokes in the left hand at all during *khālī*? If we turn once again to *tīntāl* it provides the answer:

X				2				
1	2	3	4	5	6	7	8	
dhā	dhin	dhin	dhā	dhā	dhin	dhin	dhā	
0				3				X
9	10	11	12	13	14	15	16	1 *etc.*
dhā	tin	tin	tā	tā	dhin	dhin	dhā	dhā *etc.*

Inside the box are the *bols* where the *bāyan* is not sounded. A *dhā* stroke occurs on beat 9, the beginning of *khālī*. This is a two-handed stroke. *Tin* and *tā* are sounded with the right hand only. Effectively *dhā* overlaps the *khālī vibhāg,* and *tā* overlaps *vibhāg* 3. Also *dhā* is played on the rim of the *tablā* head, giving it a sharp accented sound, making the strokes on 4, 8, 12 (to a lesser extent, because *tā* is *dhā* without the left hand) and 16 come out as accented upbeats. This has the effect of pushing the stroke pattern forward, giving the *tāl* a great sense of motion rather than being merely a repeated cycle of stressed and unstressed groups of beats.

It would be simplistic to say that a *tablā* player merely keeps time. Even before improvisation takes place the basic *thekā* is subtle and complex.

I have already stressed the importance of the voice in Indian music. This is as clearly illustrated in drumming as it is in singing or instrumental music. Complex compositions on *tablā* can be learned by memorising the *bols,* and different *bols* give a spoken representation of particular rhythmic units.

Bols are to the rhythm what *sargam* is to melody.

I have looked at the separate concepts of *rāg* and *tāl,* but to get a true picture of Indian music it is necessary to examine how these elements connect and work together in the course of a performance.

The Mogul Emperor Akbar asked his famous court musician Tansen: "How much do you know of music?"
And the reply was:
"My knowledge is like a drop in vast ocean of promise."

Rāg and tāl together

As described in Part 1, a typical performance of Indian music consists of several sections which are defined by the manner in which the melodic material of the *rāg* is explored. In the section of a performance known in instrumental music as *gat*, or in vocal music as *chīz* or *bandish*, *rāg* and *tāl* come together.

Assignment 7

12 ▢⊙

1   Listen to the tape. This is a tune based on the notes from Assignments 1–3.

Gat in tīntāl (16 beats): rāg Yaman

1 beat = ♩

2   Learn the tune – play or sing it (with *sargam* if possible).

3   Keep the *tāl* – it is in 16 beats.

4   Put the notes and the *tāl* together.

This is a *gat* in *rāg Yaman*. Notice how the significant notes of the *rāg* occur on important beats of the *tāl*. This is a feature of such compositions.

In a performance the beginning of a *gat* is signalled by the entry of the *tablā* for the first time.

When the *tablā* enters, the character of the music alters dramatically. From this point through to the end of the performance, all melodic material is subject to the strict metrical organisation of *tāl*. What happens is very much an interplay between soloist and *tablā*, with musical ideas being developed through this process. At the most basic level this takes the form of theme and variations: the *gat* is the theme which is used as the basis for improvisation.

There is another important section with *rāg* and *tāl* together. This is the *jhāllā* which is typically the climax of a performance.

38

Assignment 8

1   Listen to the tape. The *sitār* and *tablā* are playing in fast 16. Count the groups of four beats by clapping.

etc.

2   Listen to the melody which is moving slowly against the fast rhythms. These are the same melodic identity tags as in Assignments 1–3.

3   Split into two groups:

Group 1: keep the 16 (*tīntāl*).

Group 2: work with the notes of the melody, keeping in time with group 1.

In *jhāllā* the profile of the music becomes more overtly rhythmic. In the fast interplay between the main and *chikārī* strings the main melodic features stand out in slow-moving lines. Although the melody is still important, *jhāllā* is primarily about exploring rhythmic patterns within the *tāl*. For example, the *tāl* can be 'cut up' in various ways. Look at 16 again:

X   2   0   3   X
1 2 3 4 5 6 7 8 9 10 11 12 13 14 15 16 1 *etc.*

Essentially this is in four sections, each containing four beats. The first beat of each group is accented in basic *jhāllā* patterns on the *sitār*:

1 2 3 4 5 6 7 8 9 10 11 12 13 14 15 16 1 *etc.*
>   >   >   >   > *etc.*
                                                    (4 + 4 + 4 + 4)

By accenting different groupings of beats, other rhythmic effects are achieved:

```
1  2  3  4  5  6  7  8  9  10  11  12  13  14  15  16  1  etc.
>        >  >  >              >           >
                              (4 + 2 + 2 + 4 + 4)
```

```
1  2  3  4  5  6  7  8  9  10  11  12  13  14  15  16  1  etc.
>        >        >     >     >       >       >
                              (4 + 4 + 2 + 2 + 2 + 2)
```

```
1  2  3  4  5  6  7  8  9  10  11  12  13  14  15  16  1  etc.
>     >        >     >        >       >       >
                              (3 +3 + 3 + 3 + 2 + 2)
```

```
1  2  3  4  5  6  7  8  9  10  11  12  13  14  15  16  1  etc.
>     >        >  >           >          >       >
                              (3 + 3 + 2 + 3 + 3 + 2)
```

```
1  2  3  4  5  6  7  8  9  10  11  12  13  14  15  16  1  etc.
>     >        >  >        >              >       >
                              (3 + 3 + 2 + 2 + 4 + 2)
```

```
1  2  3  4  5  6  7  8  9  10  11  12  13  14  15  16  1  etc.
>              >              >        >        >
                              (5 + 5 + 3 + 3)
```

```
1  2  3  4  5  6  7  8  9  10  11  12  13  14  15  16  1  etc.
>              >                    >        >     >
                              (6 + 6 + 2 + 2)
```

Many groupings are possible. While the melody instrument is working with these permutations, the basic pattern of *tāl* is kept intact on the *tablā*, and when the *tablā* works with different permutations the melody instrument holds the *tāl*.

The *jhāllā* concludes with a cross-rhythmic cadence known as a *tihāī* played in unison by the *sitār* and *tablā*. We'll look at *tihāīs* in more detail in Part 3.

Assignment 9

1   Divide into two groups. Group 1 clap *tīntāl* (16), clapping on 1, 5 and 13.

2   While group 1 keeps *tāl*, group 2 claps on 1, 5, 9 and 13. Work on this until it is steady.

3   Next, group 2 claps a beat pattern of 4 + 2 + 2 + 4 + 4 (i.e. claps on 1, 5, 7, 9 and 13). Group 1 continues to keep *tāl* (clapping on 1, 5 and 13).

```
          1  2  3  4  5  6  7  8  9  10  11  12  13  14  15  16  1  etc.
Group 1  >           >                           >               >
Group 2  >           >     >     >               >               >
```

Work until both groups can hold their rhythmic pattern steady.

4   Continue in this way, using the other groupings of beats shown above.

5   Invent new groupings of beats that add up to 16, and work with them.

When the class is confident working in two groups with these metrical patterns, it could divide into three or four smaller groups, one keeping *tāl* while the others clap various *jhāllā* beat groupings. This is tricky, and should only be introduced when the *jhāllā* patterns are thoroughly understood. At this stage introduce a clap to every beat. This is difficult as the accents have to stand out clearly for the proper effect to be achieved.

Stage 2 of Assignment 9 is significant because it is important to understand that *khālī* is not always indicated. Only the *tablā* indicates *khālī* in *jhāllā*. However, the framework of the *tāl* should always be kept mentally.

Assignments 1–9 have explored the various stages in a typical performance of Indian classical music, isolating the important melodic and rhythmic aspects of each section. The performance falls into two larger sections:

> *Rāg* without *tāl* (see Assignments 1–3)
> *Rāg* with *tāl* (see Assignments 7–8)

In a general sense these sections are similar to movements in a piece of Western classical music inasmuch as it is through the sequence of these sections that the broad outlines of the performance can be perceived and understood.

However, the analogy with Western classical music quickly breaks down. Because Indian music is essentially improvised, the various sections may vary in length from performance to performance, with some sections even being omitted, such as the first, unaccompanied *jhāllā* (Assignment 3). However, the sequence of musical events always remains the same – *ālāp* would never follow *gat*, for example.

A schematic representation of the various sections of a performance of a *rāg* is presented on pages 44–45.

Working effectively within this musical format depends on the ability to improvise or extemporise with given melodic and metric material. The process of improvisation in Indian music is not as 'free' as it may at first appear. In Part 3 we examine that process in more detail.

Diagram of *rāg* and *tāl* in performance

Ālāp

- Melodic material of *rāg* established
- Important notes defined
- Pitch relationships established
- Extensive and detailed ornamentation
- Progressive exposition from lower to higher octaves
- Gradual increase in speed and musical density apparent

Joṛ

- Regular pulse introduced (not metre)
- Melodic material of *ālāp* re-examined and expanded
- Musical density increases
- Gradual acceleration in tempo continues

Jhāllā

- Rhythmic interplay between melody and *chikāri* strings (high-pitched drones) becomes centre of attention
- As rhythmic density increases, melodic material of *rāg* stands out in sharp relief, although more sparse in terms of amount of notes used

Rhythm free

Regular pulse

Gradual acceleration

BREAK

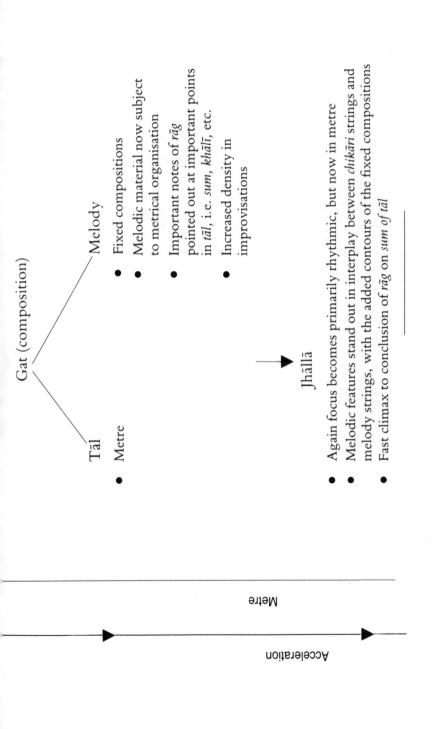

Gat (composition)

Tāl

- Metre

Melody

- Fixed compositions
- Melodic material now subject to metrical organisation
- Important notes of *rāg* pointed out at important points in *tāl*, i.e. *sum*, *khālī*, etc.
- Increased density in improvisations

Jhāllā

- Again focus becomes primarily rhythmic, but now in metre
- Melodic features stand out in interplay between *chikāri* strings and melody strings, with the added contours of the fixed compositions
- Fast climax to conclusion of *rāg* on *sum of tāl*

Metre

Acceleration

What is 'improvisation' in Indian music?

What is 'improvisation' in Indian music?

Inevitably we use the word 'improvisation' to describe much of what happens in Indian music. However, as Indian musicians often point out, this term is not strictly accurate.

The notion of improvisation in music is generally complex and often contradictory. Say 'improvisation' to a player of jazz, rock, blues, reggae, Baroque, flamenco, folk, Persian or Indian music, and they will all think of different things. What they might all share in common, however, is some concept of re-working given musical material in performance, 'on the spot'. In this sense improvisation may also be defined as instant or spontaneous composition. But that idea throws up other questions. How spontaneous is spontaneous? Can an Indian musician really perform spontaneously on the same *rāg* for one or two hours? The answer to that lies in the kind of material the musician has to work with, and what rules are in operation during performance. It is the mixture of musical permutations available, and the restrictions of the musical form, that allow the 'improvisation' to happen.

Palṭās

The key to improvising in Indian music lies in how and what musicians practise. It is only through understanding this process that improvisations can be built successfully using the materials of Indian music.

For example, we have looked at a *gat* in *Yaman*. On the next page are a set of *tāns* based on that *gat*:

Gat

G R GGḾ Ḿ   G   RG   RS S   Ṇ   RRG   Ḿ   N   D   P   Ḿ

Tāns in rāg Yaman

Tāns   4 beats of improvisation, then back to the gat

1   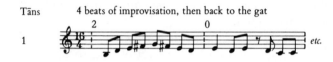   etc.

8 beats of improvisation

2      etc.

12 beats

3      etc.

16 beats

4      etc.

Tāns are typical of the sort of improvised breaks that happen in Indian music. These are basically sets of variations of ever-increasing length, but with another musical concept, known as *palṭās* or *alaṅkārs,* underlying the process.

Assignment 10

1 Listen to the tape. Here is a scale using the notes you have worked with already.

2 Now listen to the different ways the *sitār* plays up and down the scale.

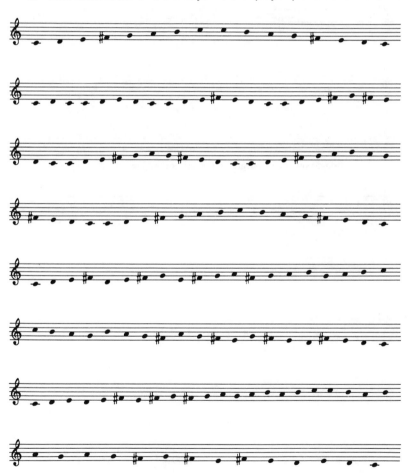

3 Learn to work with the scale in these ways.

Palṭās or *alaṅkārs* are common to both vocal and instrumental music. They are more than just practice patterns that give technical fluency to the voice or hands: they are the essential material required for improvisation in Indian music. Here is a typical set of *palṭās* in *rāg Yaman*:

Or with three notes to each degree of the scale, or four, etc.

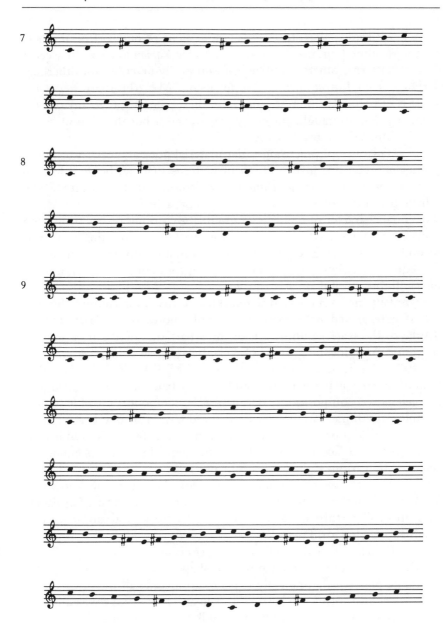

All these *palṭās* stress scalar movement of one sort or another. Although some (e.g. no. 2) are specific to *rāg Yaman* in terms of ascent/descent patterns, others could be just as usefully practised for other *rāgs* deriving from *Kalyāṇ thāt*, i.e. scales using MA (the sharpened 4th). What is of particular interest is not how these *palṭās* relate to any one *rāg* (similar *palṭās* are taught for every *rāg* anyway), but the permutational way in which the notes are treated.

This way of practising scalar material not only teaches technical proficiency but also instils a fund of patterns that can be used later in performance. For example, *palṭās* 4 to 8 demonstrate two main ways in which the notes of the scale may be approached. First, there is the sequential character of the phrases gradually working up the scale from successive degrees, which is a common way of constructing *tāns*. And second, the increasing-length rhythmic groupings implied by the melodic sequences: 3 notes, 4, 5, 6 and 7. An improvisation using this kind of idea will thus operate on at least two levels.

Palṭā no. 3 shows a different kind of rhythmic concern. Similar *palṭās* can be played in this manner, but with 3 notes, or 4, 5, 6 or 7 to each degree of the scale. Within each of these patterns there can be various rhythmic groupings, e.g. five notes can be grouped 2 + 3, 3 + 2, 1 + 4, 4 + 1, 2 + 2 + 1. Seven notes can be grouped 3 + 4, 2 + 2 + 3, etc. This kind of practice is particularly useful for constructing improvisations in *vilambit* (slow) compositions. Because of the tempo it is possible to play complex rhythmic variations within the duration of one beat. This is known as *bolbānt* or *boltāns* in vocal and instrumental music. On instruments the clear accentuation of the different rhythmic groupings is achieved by various right-hand stroke patterns.

This is also important practice for the technique known as *layakārī*, manipulating the *laya* or rhythmic flow of the music. *Layakārī* is a feature of all performances of Indian classical music, and can be heard in its most complex form in *tablā* solos.

Palṭā no. 9 shows another central concept in Indian music. This is the idea of expanding melodic motifs or shapes. Starting from two notes the range of the *palṭā* gradually expands to include all the notes of the scale. This idea forms the basis of this lengthy *tora* (improvised break) shown to me by my teacher Debu Chaudhuri. It is in *rāg Todī*.

Tora in rāg Todī

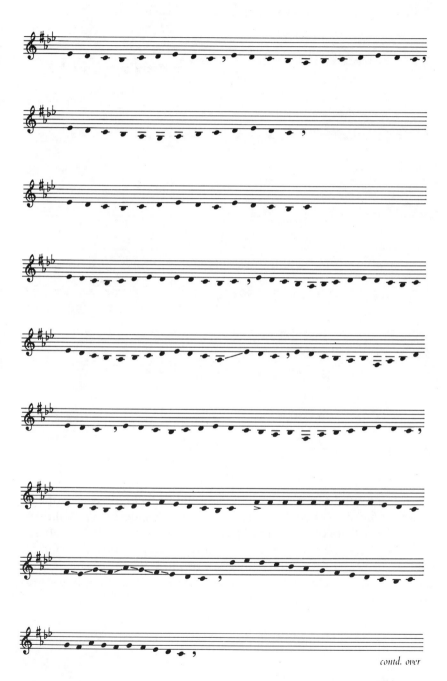

contd. over

This kind of extemporisation would probably appear in the *jor* section of the *rāg*, although the same concept can underlie *tāns* in the *gat*.

Even from these few basic *palṭās* a wealth of possibilities is offered for melodic variation. Permutation of notes is the key to all this, and the ultimate practice of this kind is to work through every possible permutation of the seven notes in the scale. For example, four notes give twenty-four permutations in all:

Permutations of four notes

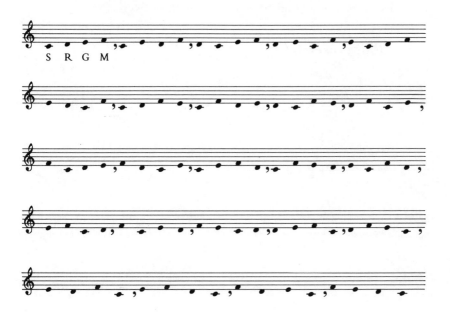

S R G M

Seven notes gives 5,040 permutations.

One of my teachers, Suresh Mishra, simply called this process practising 'the numbers'. I was left to wonder if anyone actually sat down and regularly practised all the permutations!

Of course not all *rāgs* use seven notes; there are many pentatonic *rāgs*. *Palṭās* are constructed accordingly to deal with these. For example, in *rāg Mālkauns* I was taught the following *phirat* exercises:

Phirat exercises

Phirat means to 'turn around'. These exercises take into account the inherent difficulty of sustaining interesting musical structures with scant material, i.e. five notes. They are constructed in groups of eight notes, and hence are useful for making *tāns* in *tīntāl*.

The exhaustive practice of *palṭās* is constantly emphasised in the learning of Indian music. The student spends far more time working on *palṭās* than learning compositions in different *rāgs*. *Palṭās* provide a vast fund of rhythmic patterns and melodic configurations which fall naturally under the hand or roll effortlessly off the tongue in performance. With the basic scalar material in place, adjustments are made to suit particular *rāgs*. From my own experience the melodic details of *rāgs* are not learned through *palṭās* as such but through the teaching of *ālāp*. Although *ālāp* is the first section of the *rāg* that is heard in performance, it is usually the last to be taught to the student. Because of the attention to melodic minutiae it is considered the most difficult part of the *rāg*.

These methods of practice remain the same for beginner and master. An Indian teacher would say that no-one ever reaches the state where it is no longer necessary to practise *palṭās*.

It can be useful when practising to think of three levels being involved:

1 The basic scalar material (*thāt*).
2 *Palṭās*, exercises designed to work through the various permutations (rhythmic and melodic) of the scalar material.
3 Adjustments of these permutations and patterns to suit different *rāgs*.

". . . that training is the most intricate which leads to the utter simplicity of a tune."

Tagore

Tāns

Assignment 11

16 🔘   1   Listen to the tape. The *sitār* plays a set of *tāns* (melodic variations) on a *gat* from *rāg Yaman*.

Gat

G R RG GṀ Ṁ   G RG RS S   Ṇ RRG Ṁ   N D P Ṁ

Tāns   4 beats of improvisation, then back to the gat

1

etc.

8 beats of improvisation

2

etc.

12 beats

3

etc.

16 beats

4

etc.

60

2   Learn a few of these *tāns* on instrument or voice. Memorise them. Memorise the patterns rather than the individual notes, as it is the patterns that are important – they are based on the exercises in Assignment 10. Work in two groups, with one group keeping *tīntāl* (16) while the other group plays the melodic material.

3   Try making up your own *tāns* using similar patterns.

These variations, as mentioned before, are known as *tāns*. Notice how there is a gradual expansion in the length of the variations and in their melodic range. In a performance they would not be rendered in such a simplistic manner, but the same general principle would apply: the process of increasing the length and range of the improvised material while the *gat* remains as the melodic and metric reference point.

Look again at the fourth *tān*. The group of bracketed notes is called a *tihāī* (literally, third), a thrice-played cadential pattern used to bring improvisations to a close.

These are important punctuation marks in the musical flow. *Tablā* players are particularly skilled in fashioning complex *tihāīs*.

A composer once said to me that he thought of this type of improvisation as being a process of 'submerging' the basic notes of the composition, the *gat,* and replacing them with increasingly complex variations, with the *gat* occasionally surfacing as a reference point.

The actual form these variations take in performance depends on many factors. For example, there are different styles of *gat* in instrumental music such as *Masīt Khanī* or *Raza Khanī* which refer to the tempo of the compositions and more specifically the *bol* patterns used on instruments which are particular to these *gats*. In vocal music distinction is made between *baṛā* (large) *Khyāl* and *chotā* (small) *Khyāl*, influencing the nature of the improvisation. The finer details of these technicalities need not concern us here; what is more important is to understand how melodic variations are structured within *tāl* in general terms.

When thinking about the relationship between *palṭās* and performance, an analogy with spoken language can help. The *palṭās* provide a structural grammar which can be re-worked into different 'sentences' in performance. Like all speech, Indian music is a mixture of the learned and the spontaneous. The materials of language offer endless possibilities to re-shuffle words within a grammar and still make sense. 'Improvisation' in Indian music can be seen as a comparable process.

I should not push the comparison with language too far, for in the final analysis music is structured in a very different way from language, but before leaving this line of thought let us look at the manner in which variations are generated on the *tablā* using the kinds of *bol* patterns examined earlier in Assignment 6.

Assignment 12

17

1   Listen to the tape. The *tablā* player is playing *tīntāl* (16 beats). He says a particular pattern of *bols*:

X				2			
1	2	3	4	5	6	7	8
Dhā	Dhā	Te	Te	Dhā	Dhā	Tūn	Nā

0				3			
9	10	11	12	13	14	15	16
Tā	Tā	Te	Te	Dhā	Dhā	Dhūn	Nā

2   Are these sounds different from the other sounds you learned for 16?

3   Learn the new sounds.

4   Listen to how the *tablā* player improvises with these sounds, shuffling them around in various sequences.

5   Learn this new sequence:

X				2			
1	2	3	4	5	6	7	8
Te	Te	Dhā	Dhā	Dhā	Dhā	Tūn	Nā

0				3			
9	10	11	12	13	14	15	16
Te	Te	Tā	Tā	Dhā	Dhā	Dhūn	Nā

6   Practise the original pattern, then the variation, then back to the original. Don't pause between them.

The above stroke pattern is known as a *quāidā*.

Quāidā

A *quāidā* is different from a *ṭhekā*, being used specifically as a basis for making variations rather than as a framework for keeping *tāl* when accompanying.

A *quāidā* will have various sets of *palṭās* (the word has a slightly different meaning here), which are ways of creating variations by a process of permutation of the *bols*:

1

X				2			
1	2	3	4	5	6	7	8
Te	Te	Dhā	Dhā	Dhā	Dhā	Tūn	Nā

0				3			
9	10	11	12	13	14	15	16
Te	Te	Tā	Tā	Dhā	Dhā	Dhūn	Nā

2

X				2			
1	2	3	4	5	6	7	8
Dhā	Te	Te	Dhā	Dhā	Dhā	Tūn	Nā

0				3			
9	10	11	12	13	14	15	16
Tā	Te	Te	Dhā	Dhā	Dhā	Dhūn	Nā

3

X				2			
1	2	3	4	5	6	7	8
Dhā	Dhā	Dhā	Dhā	Te	Te	Tūn	Nā

0				3			
9	10	11	12	13	14	15	16
Tā	Tā	Tā	Tā	Te	Te	Dhūn	Nā

4

X				2			
1	2	3	4	5	6	7	8
Dhā	Dhā	Dhā	Te	Te	Dhā	Tūn	Nā

0				3			
9	10	11	12	13	14	15	16
Tā	Tā	Tā	Te	Te	Dhā	Dhūn	Nā

5

X				2			
1	2	3	4	5	6	7	8
Dhā	Dhā	Te	Te	Dhā	Dhā	Tūn	Nā

0				3			
9	10	11	12	13	14	15	16
Dhā	–	–	–	Dhā	Dhā	Te	Te

X				2			
1	2	3	4	5	6	7	8
Dhā	Dhā	Tūn	Nā	Dhā	–	–	–

0				3			
9	10	11	12	13	14	15	16
Dhā	Dhā	Te	Te	Dhā	Dhā	Tūn	Nā

X
1
Dhā (returns to basic *quāidā*)

Other variations can be created, still based on the original *quāidā*:

1

X				2			
1	2	3	4	5	6	7	8
Dhā Dhā	Te Te	Dhā Dhā	Te Te	Dhā Dhā	Te Te	Dhā Dhā	Tūn Nā

0				3			
9	10	11	12	13	14	15	16
Tā Tā	Te Te	Tā Tā	Te Te	Dhā Dhā	Te Te	Dhā Dhā	Dhūn Nā

2

X				2			
1	2	3	4	5	6	7	8
Dhā Dhā	Te Te	Te Te	Te Te	Dhā Dhā	Te Te	Dhā Dhā	Tūn Nā

0				3			
9	10	11	12	13	14	15	16
Tā Tā	Te Te	Te Te	Te Te	Dhā Dhā	Te Te	Dhā Dhā	Dhūn Nā

3 X   2

1	2	3	4	5	6	7	8
Dhā Dhā	Te Te	Dhā Te	Te Dhā	Dhā Dhā	Te Te	Dhā Dhā	Tūn Nā

0   3

9	10	11	12	13	14	15	16
Tā Tā	Te Te	Tā Te	Te Tā	Dhā Dhā	Te Te	Dhā Dhā	Dhūn Nā

4 X   2

1	2	3	4	5	6	7	8
Dhā Te	Te Dhā	Dhā Te	Te Dhā	Dhā Dhā	Te Te	Dhā Dhā	Tūn Nā

0   3

9	10	11	12	13	14	15	16
Tā Te	Te Tā	Tā Te	Te Tā	Dhā Dhā	Te Te	Dhā Dhā	Dhūn Nā

5 X   2

1	2	3	4	5	6	7	8
Dhā Dhā	Dhā Dhā	Te Te	Te Te	Dhā Dhā	Te Te	Dhā Dhā	Tūn Nā

0   3

9	10	11	12	13	14	15	16
Tā Tā	Tā Tā	Te Te	Te Te	Dhā Dhā	Te Te	Dhā Dhā	Dhūn Nā

6

X				2			
1	2	3	4	5	6	7	8
Dhā Dhā	Dhā Dhā	Te Te	Te Te	Dhā Dhā	Te Te	Dhā Dhā	Tūn Nā

0				3			
9	10	11	12	13	14	15	16
Dhā –	– –	– –	– –	Dhā Dhā	Dhā Dhā	Te Te	Te Te

X				2			
1	2	3	4	5	6	7	8
Dhā Dhā	Te Te	Dhā Dhā	Tūn Nā	Dhā –	– –	– –	– –

0				3			
9	10	11	12	13	14	15	16
Dhā Dhā	Dhā Dhā	Te Te	Te Te	Dhā Dhā	Te Te	Dhā Dhā	Tūn Nā

X
1

Dhā (returns to basic *quāidā*)

This short set of *palṭās* gives some idea of the possibilities offered by such a process. Notice how the metrical material is used in various ways. In the second set not only has the speed of the strokes been doubled but metric motifs such as Dhā Dhā Te Te Dhā Dhā Tūn Nā have been compressed to fit four beats instead of eight, so they function as a continual reference point to the original structure of the *quāidā*, at the same time slotting rhythmically into the variations.

Obviously the sequences can become more complex, depending on the different strokes and metrical units employed. Other formulae for generating variations on *tablā* are *peshkār, uṭhān, ṭukrā, gat, relā*. Each of these forms has its own particular *bols*, and ways of expanding and re-working the metrical material.

As well as keeping all these patterns and combinations 'on tap', the *tablā* player will also respond spontaneously to musical ideas suggested by the soloist's improvisations. However, the ultimate displays of the rhythmic complexities offered by the *tablā* come in solo performances where the different kinds of variational processes are explored in full.

Tihāīs

In the above examples, no. 5 from the first set of variations and no. 6 from the second are *tihāīs*. These have already appeared in melodic form (page 57), but it will be worth taking a closer look at them and how they work.

Assignment 13

A *tihāī* is a rhythmic figure played three times in succession, in such a way that it finishes on the first beat of the *tāl*, or on some other important point such as *khālī* or the opening phrase of the composition. In effect a *tihāī* is a rhythmic cadence.

In this assignment we use two different *tihāīs*. Here is the first, a 9-beat *tihāī*:

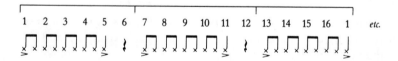

Every note in the *tihāī* should be clapped, but the accents on beats 9, 11, 12, 14, 15 and 1 are necessary to make the division of the *tihāī* into three identical rhythmic figures stand out. Note how the last beat of the *tihāī* is the first beat of the next cycle.

Here is the second *tihāī*, a 17-beat one:

This time the accents are on beats 1, 5, 7, 11, 13 and 1. Again the last beat of the *tihāī* is the first beat of the next cycle.

A 1   Work in two groups. Both groups clap *tīntāl*, but after one-and-a-half cycles together, group 2 claps the 9-beat *tihāī* while group 1 continues with *tīntāl*. Here's the second cycle:

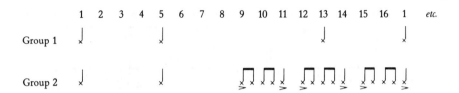

2   Work with this until both groups can hold the *tāl* and *tihāī* steady.

3   Swap the *tihāī* between groups from cycle to cycle: group 1 *tīntāl*, group 2 *tihāī*, immediately followed by group 1 *tihāī*, group 2 *tīntāl*, and so on. Do this without a pause. Don't break the cycle.

A way to end this first stage of the assignment is for both groups to play the *tihāī* together at a point indicated by the teacher. It is important that all exercises with *tāl* conclude on beat 1. In this way the cyclical nature of *tāl* is always emphasised.

B 1   Both groups clap *tīntāl*. After one cycle together, group 2 claps the 17-beat *tihāī*:

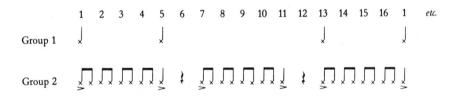

Notice how this *tihāī* has rests at beats 6 and 12.

2   Work with this *tihāī* as before, swapping groups, etc. End with both groups playing the *tihāī* and stopping on beat 1.

This exercise has a continuous effect of overlapping rhythms because the *tihāī* spans a complete cycle of 16 and overlaps onto the first beat of the next cycle.

C 1   Both groups play *tīntāl*. After one cycle together, group 1 claps the 9-beat *tihāī* (starting on beat 9 of the second cycle) and group 2 claps the 17-beat *tihāī* (starting on beat 1 of the second cycle).

Return to *tīntāl* for one cycle together, then repeat the *tihāīs*.

2   Swap *tihāīs* between groups, without stopping.

3   Both groups should end with the 17-beat *tihāī*.

Another way to work with this idea is to have three groups. One group keeps 16 while the other two play *tihāīs* as above. All three groups should end the exercise on beat 1.

Working with *tihāīs* is rhythmically exciting and demanding. It is worth persevering with such exercises because awareness of how to use *tihāīs* within *tāl* is an important feature of Indian musical structure.

Tihāīs have several important functions in the overall shape of a performance:

1   To bring a section of improvisation to a definite close.
2   To punctuate a series of different melodic ideas in improvisation. *Tihāīs* are not played after every improvised break; they are used sparingly for greater effect.
3   To make climactic cadences. This is especially important in a music where little or no structural use is made of dynamics.

Tihāīs can be fashioned starting on any beat of the *tāl*. Here are a set of *tihāīs* in *tīntāl*.

This shows how *tihāīs* can be progressively built up within one cycle of *tīntāl*. Semiquavers are used here to give a sense of movement, but any rhythmic units are suitable, depending on tempo, etc.

The way in which these *tihāīs* are worked out is quite straight-forward: take the number of beats you have to work with, depending on your starting-point in the *tāl*, and divide by three, always keeping in mind that the first beat of the next cycle is the last beat of the *tihāī*. For example, look at the *tihāī* starting on beat 6. This has twelve beats in all, and this divides conveniently into three groups of four beats. When we start from beat 5 it is a bit trickier: 13 beats are not equally divisible by three. But we can adapt the previous grouping by introducing one beat's-worth of rest distributed evenly across the *tihāī*, i.e. half-beat rests at beats 9 and 13 as shown. This principle is applied through all the examples shown. Accent is all-important in *tihāīs*, so that the groups of three stand out clearly.

Tihāīs can last more than one cycle of the *tāl*. Here is a long *tihāī* of the type often used to end a performance of a *rāg*. This *tihāī* covers 15 cycles in all.

×				2				0				3			
1	2	3	4	5	6	7	8	9	10	11	12	13	14	15	16

(musical notation — half notes grouped across the cycle)

1	2	3	4	5	6	7	8	9	10	11	12	13	14	15	16

1	2	3	4	5	6	7	8	9	10	11	12	13	14	15	16

5 cycles

1	2	3	4	5	6	7	8	9	10	11	12	13	14	15	16

1	2	3	4	5	6	7	8	9	10	11	12	13	14	15	16

1	2	3	4	5	6	7	8	9	10	11	12	13	14	15	16

1	2	3	4	5	6	7	8	9	10	11	12	13	14	15	16

1	2	3	4	5	6	7	8	9	10	11	12	13	14	15	16

5 cycles

1	2	3	4	5	6	7	8	9	10	11	12	13	14	15	16

1	2	3	4	5	6	7	8	9	10	11	12	13	14	15	16

1	2	3	4	5	6	7	8	9	10	11	12	13	14	15	16

1	2	3	4	5	6	7	8	9	10	11	12	13	14	15	16

1	2	3	4	5	6	7	8	9	10	11	12	13	14	15	16

5 cycles

1	2	3	4	5	6	7	8	9	10	11	12	13	14	15	16

1	2	3	4	5	6	7	8	9	10	11	12	13	14	15	16
													(>)	(>)	(>)	(>)

1

This *tihāi* would be played very fast, in unison by the soloist and *tablā*. Its structure is fairly simple: basically one block of five cycles of *tīntāl* played three times. Within this, other groups of notes are also played three times, implying *tihāis* within the larger *tihāīs*. Use is not made of cross-rhythms and displacement of beats as such, but the *tihāī* works because it is based on the idea of delaying the final *sum* or first beat.

The ways in which rhythmic units can be re-worked, shuffled, cut up and re-assembled is one of the most fascinating aspects of Indian music, and in music education could have many useful applications.

I have outlined how the basic materials of Indian music work and how they are used in improvisation. If the focus has been mainly on structures that are commonly found in instrumental music, this is not because instrumental music is any more important than vocal music; it certainly is not, especially in the opinion of Indian musicians themselves. Rather, instrumental music has been chosen because in terms of overall structure it has, in a sense, the best of both worlds. It is basically derived from vocal music, but also introduces other interesting musical devices that are characteristically instrumental, such as *jhāllā*. (Some vocalists would argue that everything in instrumental music has vocal antecedents. Others say that the influence now works both ways.) Also, the overall form of an instrumental performance is perhaps easier to grasp for a newcomer to the music. However, the ultimate subtleties of melodic inflection are to be found in vocal music; instruments can only approximate to them.

In any case, debates about the pre-eminence of vocal over instrumental music are not the concern of this book. More important is an understanding of how the concepts of *rāg* and *tāl* are employed in the making of music. These concepts seem unapproachable and rather complex at first, but what I have tried to show here is that they should be viewed first and foremost as a framework within which structured improvisation can take place.

It is also important to grasp the idea of improvisation as a mixture of the learned and the spontaneous, worked through within the large-scale structure of the *rāg*.

Viewed in isolation, the constituent parts of a *rāg* may seem musically sparse and uninteresting. It is only through their interaction within the large-scale structure that they become musically coherent.

From an educational point of view it is important to keep a sense of form in mind when working with the various musical materials derived from this music. Parts should not be misrepresented as the whole: the *gat* being taught in isolation from the *ālāp,* and so on. Indian music is sometimes oversimplified to the point where its educational potential is entirely lost – it becomes just a type of song with a slightly peculiar rhythm, or maybe *tīntāl* just gets reduced to 4/4.

With this in mind we can look at the possibility of composing a piece which brings together all the musical materials already explored.

74

Final assignment: Composing a piece with *rāg* and *tāl*

There are various stages to composing this piece, drawing on the work of Assignments 1–12.

Stage 1

Decide on a scale or group of notes which will form the basis of the piece. In keeping with what we have encountered, make rules about how the notes may be used in the piece: ascent/descent patterns, which notes are important, etc. Decide on a drone based on the tonic or SA of the scale plus one other important note. This drone can be held throughout the piece as a reference point, perhaps played as an ostinato:

This is the way in which the drone accompaniment is played on Indian instruments such as the *tānpūrā* (see Part 4). If played like this the drone should never be allowed to speed up. It must be an unchanging background to the music.

Stage 2

Explore the scale in the same way as in Assignments 1–3.

Stage 3

Compose a *gat* (composition) in 16 beats. Compose variations using the type of scale material used in Assignments 10 and 11. Gradually increase the speed of the composition and move into *jhāllā* patterns as shown in Assignment 9. End with a *tihāī* as in Assignment 13 (perhaps try the long 15-cycle *tihāī*! – see page 68). The *tihāī* should use the important notes of the scale.

Remember, this composition is following the sequence of sections in a performance of an Indian *rāg*:

    Ālāp – free and slow, without a regular beat
    Jor – regular pulse but no metre
    Jhāllā – introducing metrical patterns
    Gat – fixed composition in *tāl* (rhythmic cycle)
    Jhāllā – fast rhythmic climax using various ways of 'cutting up' *tāl*

Try to make each section grow out of the previous one. The melodic material should remain coherent and consistent throughout.

Any instruments can be used in this piece. Some are better for specific purposes. For example, synthesizers are useful for achieving the smooth passage between notes typical of vocal and instrumental Indian music. Stringed instruments such as violin or cello can be used effectively in this way. Classroom instruments such as tuned percussion are best utilised for defining the beat groupings and stresses of the *tāl*. If Indian instruments such as the *sitār*, harmonium and *tablā* are available, it is best to keep the SA (ground note or tonic) of the piece around C (C♯ is ideal for *sitār* and *tablā* but may be difficult for other instruments).

These are only indications of the type of functions specific instruments might perform. Experimentation will reveal other interesting ways of using the instruments to best effect.

That, then, is an attempt to compose a piece using the structure of Indian classical music. In the end it may not sound authentically like Indian music, but that need not matter. The objective is to explore Indian musical form, using it as a basis for creating structured improvisation.

Here is a summary of the various assignments.

Assignments 1–3 – exploring the melodic material of the *rāg* without *tāl*

Assignments 4–6 – exploring *tāl* alone

Assignments 7–9 – *rāg* and *tāl* together

Assignments 10–12 – exploring the way in which improvisation happens using the melodic and rhythmic materials of Indian music

In Part 4 we shall look at Indian instruments: their tuning, maintenance, and possible applications in education.

PART FOUR

The instruments of North Indian classical music

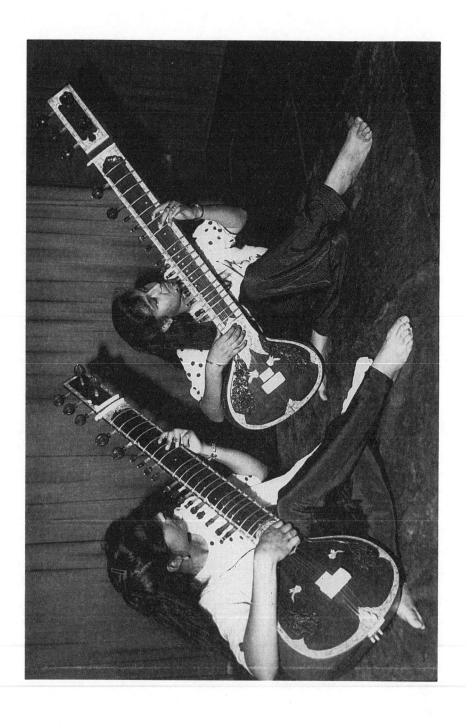

The instruments of North Indian classical music

At first glance many Indian instruments appear impossibly complicated: tiers of strings threading above and below each other, or disappearing through the holes in the neck, huge oversized frets, oddly shaped sound-boxes, long top-heavy fingerboards. The *sitār* with its 18 or 19 strings looks like some nightmarish distant cousin of the guitar. How could you strum chords on that! If a *sitār* is perceived in these terms, measured against Western instruments, then it is indeed impossible to play. But Indian music is different, and that difference is reflected both in the construction of the instruments and in their playing techniques. The *sitār* and *tablā* are not Indian equivalents of guitar and drums, but have unique musical qualities, quite distinct from those of Western instruments, which can only be fully appreciated when a good working knowledge of Indian musical structures is attained.

The purpose of this section is to explain how the main Indian instruments are held, tuned, played and maintained. Maintenance is important as Indian instruments are generally less robust than their Western counterparts, being in part constructed from materials such as dried gourds. For use in schools, considerable care is needed to keep them in good playing condition.

In describing the instruments, organological terminology has been avoided, as this is somewhat specialised and not everyone will be familiar with it. For a detailed account of Indian instruments using both Western and Indian methods of organological classification, see the Bibliography.

The instruments described here are the *sitār, sarod, tānpūrā, sāraṅgī, dilrubā, esrāj, shehnai, bansurī*, harmonium, *tablā* and *dholak*. At present the *sitār, tablā*, harmonium and *tānpūrā* are the instruments most likely to be found in (Western) schools, so a slightly more detailed description of these is given here. The others are included for their intrinsic interest, and also because they may one day come to have a larger educational role.

Stringed instruments: plucked
Sitār

In India the *sitār* dates back about 700 years, but it is thought to be Middle-Eastern in origin. Through the typically Indian process of synthesis and adaptation, the *sitār* is now archetypically Indian.

It is undoubtedly the best-known Indian instrument in the West. It was popularised in the 1950s and '60s throughout Europe and the United States, especially by Ravi Shankar. When it was taken up by the Beatles and other pop groups it became, briefly, a household word. The *sitār* was part of '60s folklore, and the '. . . magical mythical mix which combined Indian religion . . . culture and objects with hallucinogenic drugs' (David Reck, in an article in *Asian Music*, 1985). This was a curiously Western interpretation of the aesthetic/spiritual dimension in Indian music; Indian musicians certainly did not consider drug-taking an aid to playing or understanding the music, and indeed viewed it as a positive hindrance. Yet even today the *sitār* still has flower-power connotations for children not even born then. Recently when I was giving a *sitār* lesson to a thirteen-year-old he surprised me by suddenly asking, 'Didn't the Beatles play one of these?'

The '*sitār* explosion', as Ravi Shankar called it, did not last long, and pop fashions soon moved on, but the *sitār* had made its way into Western musical consciousness. Its popularity catalysed a growth of interest in traditional forms of North Indian classical music, and the *sitār*'s unique sound is still occasionally heard embedded within the complex productions of present-day pop.

One can understand why the *sitār* found favour in the West, and especially in the world of pop music. Superficially it resembles the guitar, and has an almost 'electric' sound quality in its capacity for bending and sustaining notes. Also, the modality of Indian music and its concern with melody and rhythm is, at least on the surface, closer to the world of rock and pop than the Western classical tradition. However, as many guitarists soon discovered, the *sitār* is a very different type of instrument.

Like all Indian instruments (apart from the harmonium, which is a Western import), the *sitār* is not designed for playing harmonies or chords, which have no significance in the structure of Indian music. On the *sitār* you can play melody, drone and rhythm, and the strings are set out accordingly. But first let us look at how to sit and hold a *sitār*. The illustration opposite shows the correct sitting and playing position for the *sitār*.

○   The sound box should rest on the left foot, not on the floor.
○   The *sitār* is held in place by the right knee, right forearm and left foot. It should never be supported by the left hand, which must be free to move on the neck of the instrument.

81

○   It is only possible to hold a *sitār* in this manner whilst seated on the floor. Sitting on a chair and holding it like a guitar is possible but extremely awkward.

○   When playing the *sitār* it is best to wear trousers or a long loose skirt. It is impossible to hold correctly in a tight skirt.

The notes on a *sitār* are obtained by pressing down the string just before the fret, the thumb always staying behind the neck:

The string is plucked by the index finger of the right hand, which wears a *mizrab* (wire plectrum), in a combination of up and down strokes called *bols*. The thumb on the right hand should always stay fixed in the position shown opposite.

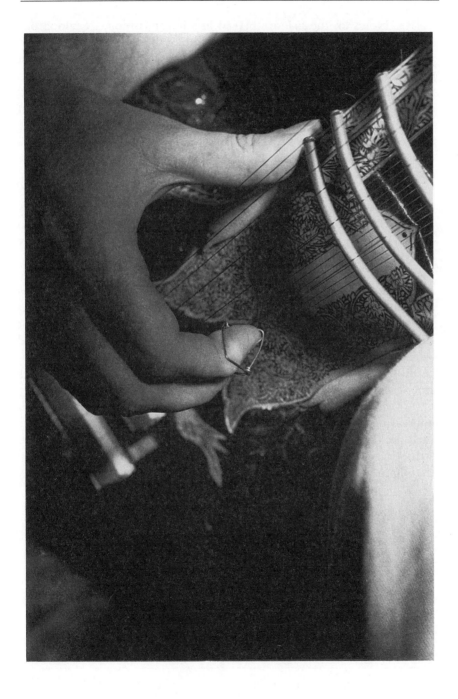

Notes on the *sitār* are played in a linear fashion, i.e. along one string rather than across the fingerboard like the guitar. (Occasionally you can play across the first two or three strings on the first few frets, but this has very limited application.) Melody on the *sitār* is played mainly on the first string. Generally only the index and middle finger of the left hand are used for fretting, and of these mainly the index: 'The constant use of one finger creates the Indian vocal legato quality, and the distance between frets is too great for much use of positional fingering.' (*Grove's Dictionary of Musical Instruments*, p. 398) The middle finger tends to take the highest note in a given phrase, with the index finger staying in place behind it. Frets 8 and 14 can be moved down for RE *komal* (flat) and DHA *komal* respectively. Frets 18, 19 and 20 are movable for RE *komal*, GA *komal* and MA *tivra* (sharp). All frets on the *sitār* are fixed by strong nylon or yarn twine, so they are adjustable for fine tuning. Some *sitārs* may only have 19 frets.

The number of strings and tuning is not standardised, and there are several systems in operation, so *sitārs* obtained for teaching purposes may vary in this respect. The musical and stylistic identity of a particular *sitār* player is often indicated by the type of instrument and tuning he or she uses. For example, two of the predominant *sitār* types are represented by Vilayat Khan and Ravi Shankar. However, these divisions should not be thought of as rigid, as there is also a great mingling of *sitār* styles amongst contemporary players.

The three most common tunings are shown below. Here as in all musical examples, SA is represented by C. The actual pitch of SA is variable, determined by the singer or instrumentalist according to such factors as vocal range, string tension, etc. On the *sitār*, the SA may be anywhere from B to D, but no higher or lower.

Sitār tunings

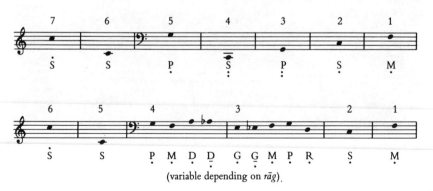

(variable depending on *rāg*).

Taraf (sympathetic) strings – tuning depends on *rāg*
In *rāg Bilawal*:

Each string or set of strings on a *sitār* is used for a specific musical purpose. This is a feature common to Indian stringed instruments but largely absent in modern Western instruments (it is found in some medieval and Renaissance instruments because of the relatively modal character of that music). Understanding the interrelation of the string functions illuminates the various sections of a *sitār* performance; on one level these represent successive explorations of the musical resources offered by the instrument. Let us look at this idea in more detail, starting with the strings and their functions.

First or main string This is used in every section of the *rāg* as the main melody string. It is the only string on the *sitār* that is consistently used for this purpose. It runs halfway across the neck, so that space is left for *mīnd* – lateral deflection of the string – which is a central feature of *sitār* playing. The largest intervals with *mīnd* can be played on the first string – hence its prominence in the *ālāp* or opening section of the *rāg*.

Second string Used both as a drone and playing string, though this latter function is limited to the first four frets or so. Its main function is to provide a SA drone to the main string, i.e. when the first string is stroked the second is also sounded.

Third and fourth strings Used either as drones or playing strings, depending on the type and tuning of the *sitār*.

Fifth string Drone only, never fretted.

85

Six and seventh strings Known as *chikāri* strings, they are never fretted and do not run over the frets, but are raised on separate bridges at the side of the neck. They are high-pitched strings, stroked in rhythmic interplay with the first string, and they play an important structural role in various sections of the *rāg*.

Sympathetic strings Known as *taraf* strings, these resonate in sympathy with the other playing strings. They run under the frets and the main bridge, over a separate smaller bridge. They are tuned to the notes of the *rāg* being played, and are often stroked at the beginning of a performance to indicate this. Also, occasionally the little finger of the left hand strikes the nearest *taraf* strings under the frets to make rhythmic accents. These strings vary in number on different *sitārs* from 11 to 13. It is the shimmering quality of the *taraf* strings, rich in overtones and harmonics, that gives the *sitār* its characteristic and unmistakable sound.

In a *sitār* performance only the drones and sympathetic strings are always present. This is how the string functions relate to the sequence of a *rāg* performance:

Ālāp: Concentrates on single string work, predominantly the first string with extensive use of *mīnd*. *Chikāri* strings are used to punctuate ends of phrases.

Jor and *jhāllā*: These two sections, still unaccompanied, introduce a definite pulse through use of the *chikāri* strings in conjunction with the first string. In *jhāllā* this interplay of strings is taken a step further with elaborate cross-rhythmic improvisations between *chikāri* and first string known as *lārī* and *thonk*.

Gat: In this section the *sitār* is accompanied by *tablā*, and again there is a sequence of improvisations which exploit the possibilities offered by the morphology of the instrument, from single-string *vistar* to cross-rhythmic *chand*, *boltān*, *tarparan* and *tāns*, the last being fast linear melodic figures spanning the length of the neck.

Jhāllā: Finally the climax of the *rāg* concentrates on fast interplay between *chikāri* and first string.

Playing the *sitār* thus differs substantially from the approach used with a Western instrument. It also offers a model of how to improvise with melody and rhythm – the structure of the instrument gives us clear guidelines on working with this idea.

Maintenance is discussed later (page 106).

Baba had always been a strict disciplinarian with his students but he had imposed upon himself an even stricter code of conduct when he was a young man, often practising sixteen to twenty hours a day, doing with very little sleep, and getting along with the minimum of material things. Sometimes, when he practised, he tied up his long hair with a heavy cord and attached an end of the cord to a ring in the ceiling. Then, if he happened to doze while he practised, as soon as his head nodded, a jerk on the cord would pull his hair and awaken him.

Ravi Shankar, *My music, my life*

Sarod

The *sarod* is the other main plucked instrument played in North Indian classical music. The *sarod* differs from the *sitār* in many respects, and is a great contrast in both appearance and sound. It is made of one hollowed-out piece of wood with a skin table and metal-plate fingerboard. There are no frets. The strings are plucked with a large plectrum held between the thumb and index finger of the right hand. The plectrum is made of either coconut shell or wood. The *sarod*, like many North Indian instruments, has its origins in the Middle East, and it is closely related to the *rebab,* a lute-type instrument found in Afghanistan and Persia.

As there are no frets on the *sarod*, the technique of *mīnd* is achieved by sliding on the string (*ghasīt*), rather than lateral pulling. The problems of intonation are similar to those of the violin or cello. There are two ways of stopping the notes with the left hand: by pushing down with the fingertips, or by actually pushing down on the fingernail (don't grimace!) and sliding in that way. With the latter method a v-shaped groove is eventually cut into the fingernails of the index and middle fingers of the left hand – the sure sign of a dedicated *sarod* player! Rather than being merely different techniques, these two ways of playing represent two distinct stylistic schools of *sarod*. In the present day these are personified in the playing of Ali Akbar Khan (fingertips), and Amjad Ali Khan (fingernails). The two methods of playing are quite different in technical possibilities and musical effect.

Two *sarod* types are associated with these styles. They have different tunings and number of strings (see over).

87

Sarod

Sarod tunings

plus 11–15 *taraf* strings tuned to the notes of the *rāg*

plus 11–15 *taraf* strings tuned to the notes of the *rāg*

Again there is the typical layout of melody, drone and rhythm strings. As on *sitār*, most of the playing is of a linear nature on one string, but more use is made of playing across the neck.

A *sarod* performance has the same format as a *sitār* performance. Sometimes the *sarod* and *sitār* are heard together as a duet, *jugalbandi*, notably with Ravi Shankar and Ali Akbar Khan. The *sarod*'s SA is usually around B flat, so the *sitār*'s tuning has to be adjusted accordingly.

Tānpūrā

The function of the *tānpūrā* is to provide a drone accompaniment for the main melody instrument or voice. Although it resembles the *sitār* in size and shape, it is played in a very different manner. The *tānpūrā* (also spelt *tāmbūrā*) is a long-necked lute with a gourd for the sound box. It has no frets and usually has from four to six strings.

The *tānpūrā* is held vertically with the right hand plucking (or, more accurately, stroking) the strings from left to right (highest to lowest). Like the *sitār* the *tānpūrā*'s bridge is angled in such a way as to allow the string to vibrate against it giving a shimmer of resonant harmonics. On the *tānpūrā* this effect is ingeniously enhanced by placing pieces of thread under each string on the bridge. These threads are essential for the resonance and continuity of the sound.

A story concerning Tansen and his *tānpūrā* illustrates this. It was said that the *tānpūrā* that Tansen used to accompany his marvellous

Tānpūrā

singing was very old, inlaid with pearl, and extremely valuable. One day
when travelling alone he was set upon by robbers. Seeing the beautiful
tānpūrā they demanded that he hand it over. Tansen explained to them
that the soul of the instrument and the secret of its heavenly sound lay in
the threads beneath the strings. Eventually the robbers ran off with the
threads, believing that this would make them into musicians as great as
Tansen. The cunning Tansen continued safely on his way with the
tānpūrā.

The tuning of a typical four-string *tānpūrā* is:

This tuning varies depending on the notes of the *rāg* being
performed. For example, a *rāg* which does not have the note PA in it
requires that the *tānpūrā* is re-tuned accordingly, with another important
note being substituted. SA is always present.

The *tānpūrā* is played at the same speed and rhythm throughout
the performance. The tempo must not change in different sections of the
rāg. This can be difficult in sections where the other instruments are
playing fast. In vocal music the role of the *tānpūrā* is particularly
important as the singer will use it to pitch his or her notes. In instrumental
music it is possible to manage without it as most instruments have their
own drone strings.

I have already mentioned that the *tānpūrā* strings should be
stroked. This is important; if they are plucked too hard they go quickly
out of tune. So the fingers should glide lightly from string to string.

The sound of a *tānpūrā* is immediately recognisable. Nothing else
sounds quite like it, and the harmonium should not be thought of as a
substitute, although it is often used as one. Although the functions of the
tānpūrā are limited (it cannot play melody, for example), it is always a
sonorous and beautiful addition to any Indian music ensemble. It does not
require great skill to play, but it is an important and integral part of the
sound.

Modern *tānpūras* vary both in shape and size – and hence in sound
– so this should be taken into consideration when purchasing.

Stringed instruments: bowed

Sāraṅgī

The *sāraṅgī* is the foremost bowed instrument in North Indian classical music, so it may seem surprising that it only recently became known as a solo concert instrument.

One reason for this is that in the past the *sāraṅgī* was best known as an accompanying instrument for dancing-girls, and acquired an unsavoury connection with prostitution. In 1984 a conference in Delhi entitled 'The women music-makers of India' celebrated the contribution made by women, especially singers, to the growth of Indian classical music. The link between prostitution (often enforced prostitution) and music was underlined, and also the fact that it was often only within this social milieu that women were able to perform at all. (There is an interesting parallel here with female blues and jazz singers in similar social situations.) So the *sāraṅgī*'s reputation stuck, not only preventing it from being acceptable as a classical solo instrument but also putting off musicians from taking it up seriously (see bibliography).

As noted in Part 1, the *sāraṅgī* is musically the ideal instrument for accompanying the voice, but it has now been largely supplanted by the harmonium in this role. This is mainly due to the fact that the harmonium is easier to play; musically it is less flexible and expressive than the *sāraṅgī* in every respect. However, the *sāraṅgī* can nowadays be heard in solo concert performances, particularly through the efforts of Ram Narayan, in whose hands the full potential of this instrument's eloquent musical voice is realised.

Unfortunately it is unlikely that a *sāraṅgī* (or teacher) would be available in a school or college, but various aspects of the playing technique are still of interest.

The *sāraṅgī* is constructed from one piece of wood with a goat-skin sound table (like the *sarod*). The waisted sides, which help facilitate the bow movements, are typical of North Indian bowed instruments. The *sāraṅgī* has no frets. The strings are played by deflecting them to the side and pushing with the fingernail just on the cuticle. By sliding in this manner different tones are obtained. The sound is mellifluous and vocal in character. *Sāraṅgī* technique is extremely difficult, and (as noted in Part 1) often painful! The *sāraṅgī* has three heavy gut main playing strings and up to thirty-six sympathetic strings.

Sāraṅgī

Dilrubā and esrāj

The *dilrubā* has perhaps the most romantic and exotic name of any musical instrument, meaning 'robber of the heart'! The *esrāj* is basically the same kind of instrument but is slightly smaller and is predominantly found in Bengal.

These instruments have frets, and a convex neck similar to the *sitār*. The notes are stopped in the same way, except that sliding on the string replaces lateral pulling. Again there is a skin sound table. However, there is one striking difference between these and other Indian instruments: guitar-like machine-heads are used for tuning the main strings. Both instruments have four main playing strings plus two *chikāri* strings and fifteen or more sympathetic strings.

Dilrubā and esrāj tunings

plus *taraf* strings tuned to the notes of the *rāg*

Nowadays the *dilrubā* and *esrāj* are usually played with a cello bow.

The main function of the *dilrubā* and *esrāj* has always been as an accompaniment to the voice. For the *esrāj* in Bengal this is particularly the case in the large body of songs composed by Rabindrinath Tagore and known collectively as *rabindrasangīt*. This music played an important part in the Indian independence movement; the national anthem is a Tagore song. However, both the *dilrubā* and *esrāj* are also used to play classical music. One West Bengali *esrāj* player, R. Roy, has modified his instrument to give it a bigger and more resonant sound, so as to be more suitable as a solo concert instrument. The instrument he has created looks somewhat different, the peg box being like that of a *sarod*, but it is capable of all the subtle nuances and timbres of classical music. It is proof that Indian instruments, far from being fixed and ancient as sometimes assumed in the West, are in a continual state of change and adaptation.

Dilrubās and *esrājs* can usually be purchased from Indian music stockists in the West. They are certainly more common than the *sārangī* and therefore have more possibilities of application in music education. They are also somewhat less daunting to play.

94

Dilrubā (being played) and esrāj

Mention should also be made here of the Western violin in Indian music. Apart from the harmonium it is the only other Western instrument that is used widely for playing classical music, especially in South India. Of course guitars, drums, synthesizers, etc. are common in pop music. Violins have been played in Indian classical music for several hundred years, and tuning and holding–position have been altered to suit. Sometimes the violin is held against the chest (like the folk fiddle), and tuned EBEB (or variants) to expedite the use of drones. It is also occasionally held like the *sārangī* or *esrāj*, i.e. vertical to the body. Although more common in Carnatic (South Indian) music, there are several fine exponents of the violin in the North, notably V. G. Jog.

Only a few cello-players currently work in the Indian classical music tradition. However, the cello does seem to present untapped potential for playing Indian music, as was pointed out by the great *sitār* and *surbahar* (bass *sitār*) virtuoso Ustad Imrat Khan, who composed a piece for it.

Ultimately Western stringed instruments are limited for playing Indian music, mainly because of the shape of the bridges and other details of construction.

Wind instruments

Shehnai

The *shehnai* is a double-reed instrument rather like the shawm or oboe. It does not have mechanical keys but is played by stopping seven finger holes, with one or two other holes used to adjust the pitch by stopping with wax. Microtones and other subtleties of pitch are obtained by manipulation of the finger pads.

The *shehnai* has a loud, strident sound that carries well, and traditionally it is played on ceremonial occasions such as weddings and festivals, which are often outdoors. It used to be played at the city gateways to welcome important visitors. The *shehnai* was included in many of the music ensembles of the Mogul courts.

Like the *sārangī*, this instrument has only comparatively recently made its way into the field of classical concert performance. This has been due to Bismillah Khan, who is the leading exponent of shehnai in India today. He plays the full classical form on the instrument, and is renowned for the dexterity and depth of his playing. He has also played in duets with *sitār* and with violin.

Shehnai

Bansurī

The *shehnai* is usually accompanied by a smaller version of the instrument which provides a drone. There can be one or more of these accompanying *shehnais*. Great breath control is required to play the *shehnai* and the technique of circular breathing is utilised (breathing in through the nose while using a pocket of air held in the cheeks to keep playing the instrument).

The *shehnai* is made of wood with a metal bell. *Shehnais* are inexpensive and easily available in the West.

Bansurī

The Indian flute comes with many different names, but *bansurī* is the most common in the North. The flute has a long and illustrious history in India, both in music and mythology. It is the instrument of Krishna, and as such is imbued with magical and seductive powers.

There are several types of flute of varying size, range and construction. The concert flute is made of bamboo with six to eight finger holes, and can be 1–2½ feet in length. It is a transverse flute, although simpler *bansurīs* are end-blown.

The large *bansurī* is perfectly suited to playing Indian classical music. Its flexibility of tone and range is similar to the human voice and exemplifies the vocal qualities so prized in Indian music. In recent times the greatest classical master of the flute was the late Pannalal Ghosh, and he was responsible for bringing it recognition as a concert instrument. The flute is now widely played in classical music by many fine artists.

Harmonium

Since its introduction by missionaries in the last century, the harmonium has become an indispensable part of the Indian music scene. It is now by far the most common accompaniment for vocal music, having supplanted the *sāraṅgī,* and there are also harmonium soloists. Yet the harmonium still generates more controversy in Indian music circles than any other facet of music-making.

The main objection to the harmonium is that, as a fixed pitch instrument, it is incapable of producing the subtleties and ambiguities of tone so essential in Indian music. As Sorrell puts it:

> A keyboard cannot produce a true slur or portamento, nor can it produce notes other than that on the keyboard, and twelve to the octave is really a sadly restricted palette. Thus the finer nuances of Indian music are denied. (Sorrell and Narayan, 1980: 37)

As we have seen, other Indian instruments have great flexibility of melodic delivery. Such was the resistance to the harmonium that it was banned until fairly recently by All India Radio. But despite the arguments about its suitability and quality of sound, the harmonium is as popular as ever with Indian musicians, and this is ultimately the acid test of any instrument's relevance. (It is interesting to compare this with similar controversies in the West, for instance the dismay of music purists in the face of the ever-increasing popularity of electronically synthesized sound and digital sampling devices – the fear that the skills required for playing 'real' instruments may be lost.)

The Indian harmonium is a small portable instrument that is played by working a bellows with one hand. The range is usually two or three octaves. Harmoniums vary in size and sophistication, and different numbers of stops and couplers may be present. The harmonium also has an important role as a tuning reference: musicians may refer to SA for a particular piece as being *ek safed* (one white) or *ek kaalaa* (one black), referring to C or C♯ respectively. (Of course, other notes are also possible for SA.)

The harmonium is found in all types of Indian vocal music including *Khyāl, Ṭhumṛi, Qawwalī, Ghazals* and *Bhajans,* and is also used to accompany solo *tablā* and dance.

Although the popularity of the harmonium and the aesthetics of its sound will doubtless continue to inspire fierce debates among musicians, it is clearly here to stay, and has an important place in Indian music education.

Drums

Tablā

The *tablā* seem to have been present in North India since the eighteenth century and are derived from several other types of drums in existence at the time, such as the *nagarā* and *pakhāwaj*. They are now established as the most important drums for accompaniment of both vocal and instrumental music, and are also, without doubt, the most important Indian drums used in music education.

The name *tablā* refers to a set of two drums played with the right and left hands. Each drum also has a separate name: the right (higher pitched) is the *tablā* and the left the *bāyan*. They are also sometimes known as *dāhinā* (right) and *duggi* (left). The body of the *tablā* is made of a spherical piece of wood, and the *bāyan* of chromed copper or occasionally clay. The heads are goatskin with a black spot, *gab*, which is made of a dried paste made from various substances such as iron oxide ash, flour or rice paste, and soot. The thongs are made of buffalo hide.

The *tablā* sit on two cloth rings so that they can be angled into comfortable playing positions. These rings are essential as the two drums are not balanced without them. Tuning can be adjusted in two ways. The main way is by striking the thongs on the rim with a hammer to lower or raise the pitch. The other way is by moving the rounded wooden blocks that are placed between the thongs on the *tablā*. These are not usually present on the *bāyan* but sometimes round metal rings are used. The tuning of the *tablā* is more finely adjusted than that of the *bāyan*. The *tablā* should be tuned to SA to correspond with the voice or melody instrument. The *bāyan* is usually only tuned to a suitable tension, rather than to a specific note.

The complex art of playing the *tablā* differs in many ways from Western drumming. Each part of the drum head on the tablā has a particular sound, and it is the skilful interlocking of these different sounds by various combinations of finger strokes that makes *tablā* playing so unique.

In Parts 2 and 3 we looked at *bols* (strokes). This mnemonic system consists of names that relate to single right-hand strokes and combinations of right and left. The strokes are 'open' (allowed to ring) or 'closed' (damped). Open strokes on the *tablā* tend to be on the outer and middle ring of the head, and closed strokes on the black spot. Strokes with the right hand are usually played by the index and middle fingers with the annular ('ring') finger resting in place on the skin. On the *bāyan*

Tablā

the strokes alternate between index and middle fingers and flat-handed strokes.

The exact details of these stroking patterns may vary considerably because, as in all aspects of Indian music, there are many different styles and regional variations. A particular style of *tablā* playing is known as a *bāj*, hence Delhi *bāj*, Lucknow *bāj*, and so on. Each *bāj* will consist of a particular repertoire of compositions, variations and stroking techniques.

The *tablā* are usually heard in an accompanying role where the player is expected not only to keep the basic time structure through the *ṭhekā* but also to interact with the flow of the improvisations and take short 'solos' consisting of pieces such as *tukrās, parans* and *palṭās* (see Part 3). During *tablā* solos the basic time cycle is kept by the melody instrument.

There is also a tradition of solo *tablā* playing. Although less frequently performed outside India, it is in solo playing that the ultimate rhythmic complexity of the art can be heard. The *tablā* are accompanied by a melody instrument which plays a *lahrā* – a repeated melodic composition – the purpose of which is to delineate the *tāl*. The *lahrā* is often played on the *sāraṅgī*, or nowadays on harmonium or even *sitār* (indeed any melody instrument can fulfil this role). Over this repeated melody the *tablā* play sets of rhythmic variations of ever-increasing complexity, returning every so often to the basic *ṭhekā* pattern.

The *tablā* have so many applications in Indian music – from religious devotional music through to *bhangra* – that they are essential in the context of music education. *Tablā* are probably more readily available than any other Indian instrument (apart from the harmonium), and usually at a modest price.

Dholak

The *dholak* or *dholki* is nowadays used almost exclusively in folk and light forms of Indian music. However, it has an historical connection with classical music, being a forerunner of the *tablā,* and various finger strokes on the *tablā* derive from *dholak* technique.

Dholaks now feature in many types of contemporary Indian music although they would not be seen on the classical music concert platform.

That concludes this brief outline of the main instruments of North Indian classical music. Of course there are many others that could be mentioned, but they are unlikely to be available in schools.

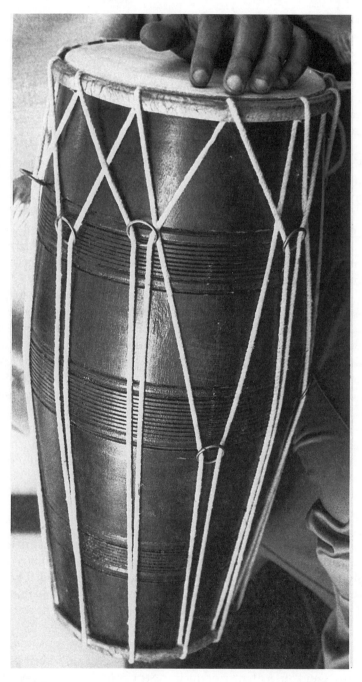

Dholak

Teaching Indian instruments

For teaching purposes all the above instruments have differing relevance and applications. The *sitār* is not suitable for younger children: is is too large and heavy to be held, and the playing action is painful to the fingers. Smaller *sitārs* are sometimes available, but they are usually not playable instruments and are more like toys. The *tablā*, however, can be learnt by children from an early age. The harmonium, also, can be used across a wide age range. The *tānpūrā* is easy to use as a drone instrument, and it does not require great skill to make an acceptable sound. Instruments such as the *dilrubā* and *esrāj* will probably be confined to secondary education for much the same reasons as the *sitār*.

For students learning either melodic or rhythm instruments it is essential that they play regularly together. The interaction of *rāg* and *tāl* is so central a feature of Indian music that it is fairly useless to learn *sitār* in isolation from *tablā* or vice versa. Performances on non-Western instruments can now be offered for GCSE.

Environment is a crucial element in playing Indian instruments. Most are played seated on the floor (though this is not strictly necessary for *shehnai* or *bansurī*), so a suitable space is required. It should have a carpeted floor and enough room to accommodate the long necks of *sitārs* and *tānpūrās* (too often *sitārs* are damaged against the walls in cramped practice rooms). The limited space and resources of many schools may not allow a specific room for Indian music activities, but a minimum standard of provision is required if Indian music is to take place at all. No one would expect an orchestra to play standing up and without music-stands; similarly no one should expect *sitār* players to sit on chairs – or hurt their ankles sitting on the hard wooden floor of a cramped room with a piano towering ominously above them.

Maintenance

Indian instruments are extremely fragile, being constructed from materials such as dried gourds and goatskin. They are damaged all too easily. Also they have many detachable parts – thin wooden pegs, tied frets, etc. So it is essential for music teachers to know something about their maintenance.

Strings These come in different gauges (see Appendix). They should be bought in rolls and cut to length, as sets of individual strings are expensive and often of inferior quality. Strings for instruments such as the *sitār, sarod* and *tānpūrā* are fixed by making small loops which fit over posts

106

and then connect to pegs. This is a fairly simple operation after a few tries. Sympathetic strings are a bit more tricky as they have to be threaded through holes in the neck, pulled through with a wire hook and then connected to the peg. Bending and pulling strings is an integral part of playing Indian instruments, so it is essential that they are kept in good condition and at the right pitch; strings that are too tight will snap when pulled.

Frets Frets on North Indian instruments are not fixed and have to be movable for adjustments to tuning. When instruments are played a lot the frets quickly loosen and sometimes come off altogether. The best material available for tying frets is nylon fishing line of medium thickness. Ordinary cotton, or even the extra-strong variety, will not do the job.

Bridges The bridges of the *sitār* and *tānpūrā* should be fixed in position with a light wood glue. They can be removed with a slight tap, but must be re-glued before being re-strung (otherwise on a *sitār* the bridge will move when the strings are pulled sideways). Another important feature of *sitār* and *tānpūrā* bridges is the *jawari*. This is the angle of curvature over the surface of the bridge. This is very slight but it gives the instruments their characteristic buzzing sound by allowing the strings to vibrate against the surface of the bridge. The bridge is made of bone, and over a period of time the strings cut grooves into it so that the *jawari* becomes dull, the string ceases to vibrate, and the life goes out of the sound. The bridge needs then to be re-filed to the proper angle. This needs to be done fairly regularly, and is a skilled job as too deep an angle will ruin the sound of the instrument. An expert on Indian instruments has to be consulted for this job; it is not really possible to do it alone without risking damage to the instrument.

The bridges on the *sarod, esrāj* and *dilrubā* are free-standing, held in place by the tension of the strings.

Reeds Tuning reeds in the harmonium is a skilled job and must be done by a specialist. Reeds for the *shehnai* can be cut to size in rather the same manner as oboe reeds.

Drum heads On the *tablā* the drum heads are easily torn or split and the black spot can become cracked and peel off. If a *tablā* head is broken a new head has to be bought – it is not really possible to repair it. However, cracks and holes in the black spot can be temporarily repaired by dabbing on nail-varnish and letting it harden. Replacing the whole head is a difficult job and should be left to the *tablā* teacher or music shop.

The life of a *tablā* head will be greatly increased if talcum powder is spread on it when playing. This helps to keep the head free from finger marks. The protective cushions usually provided with *tablā* should always be tied to the heads when the drums are not in use.

It goes without saying that all instruments should be kept in sturdy cases – not always that easy to find for Indian instruments.

If all these basic hints are followed, instruments should stay in a usable condition. There are a number of schools where *sitārs* and other instruments gather dust in dark storerooms, not because there is a lack of enthusiasm for playing them but merely because no one knows how to change a string or a fret. That is a sad waste of resources.

Conclusion

Although an attempt has been made here to explore various facets of Indian musical form, in many respects I have only touched the surface, perhaps giving a flavour of the depths of complexity inherent in the music.

The assignments are guidelines on how the structure of Indian music may be approached practically in schools. The results will not sound like Indian classical music, and that is not the intention. The aim is to build musical forms and structures, to create musical order in a way that is derived from Indian music. I have not tried to copy the characteristic nuances and subtleties of an Indian music performance (this is often impossible with Western instruments anyway), but neither have I reduced Indian music to a few simple formulae. The assignments work with the basic structural features of the music, so they should be backed up with plenty of listening to the 'real thing', i.e. performances of Indian classical music (see Discography).

For those who may wish to be performers of Indian classical music on Indian instruments, another path lies ahead.

Once, a ruler, a Maharaja, wished to hear the most beautiful music in the world, so he ordered his soldiers to kidnap the greatest musician from a neighbouring state. When the terrified musician was brought before the ruler he was ordered to sing the most beautiful *rāg* he knew but, as the musician sang, the Maharaja found that the music did not move him; indeed he felt irritated and cheated by it. In a rage he ordered the musician to be thrown into prison and executed at a later date. A few days later a soldier came and told the ruler that the musician was singing, alone, in his cell. The ruler went down to the cell and listened quietly outside the door. The musician was singing a *rāg* so full of pain, loss and longing that the ruler stayed outside for a long time, enraptured by the music. Indeed it was the most beautiful music he had ever heard. Tears rolled down the ruler's cheeks. Full of remorse he ordered that the musician should be set free at once and sent home.

Appendix

Gauges of wire used for sitār strings

1st string	Gauge 3 steel wire
2nd string	Gauge 0.335 phosphor bronze
3rd string	Gauge 7 phosphor bronze
4th string	Gauge 11 phosphor bronze
5th string	Gauge 1 steel wire
6th string	Gauge 0 steel wire
7th string	Gauge 00 steel wire
Sympathetic strings	Gauge 00 steel wire

Stringing methods may vary, but this range of gauges should cover most possibilities. Wire can be bought in 25 gm rolls from stockists of piano or harpsichord wire, and it is more economical to buy it like this than as individual strings or sets of strings.

Glossary

Alaṅkār   Scalar practice pattern.

Ālāp   Introductory section of a *rāg* in which the characteristic phrases, note relationships and ascent/descent patterns of the *rāg* are explored in detail. It is slow and unmetred, improvised within the rules of the *rāg* being played.

Anterā   The second section of a composition which usually moves into the highest octave.

Āroha   Ascending order of notes in a *rāg*.

Āvaroha   Descending order of notes in a *rāg*.

Barā   Large, great. Refers in *Khyāl* to a slow composition where the *rāg* is explored in *ālāp* fashion within the context of a composition with *tāl* (metre). Can be played in this style on instruments also.

Baṛhat   The concept of growth or expansion of musical material in a performance.

Bhajan   Religious song.

Bīn   North Indian plucked stringed instrument.

Bols   The names given to strokes used on instruments, e.g. on *sitār* Da – upstroke, Ra – downstroke. *Bols* are also used on *tablā* but are denoted by sounds such as Dhā, Dhin, Tā, etc. *Bols* work both as a memory aid and form of notation.

Boltān   *Tān* (variation) concentrating on the use of *bols,* i.e. rhythmic in emphasis.

Chikāri   High-pitched strings of *sitār* and other instruments. Tuned in octaves, and used in rhythmic interplay with the main melody strings.

Chīz   Fixed composition in *tāl* (in *Khyāl*).

Chotā   Small. Used in *Khyāl* to denote fast compositions.

Dhrupad   Genre of North Indian classical vocal music.

Drut   Fast. Describes compositions in instrumental music.

Gamak   Generic term for ornamentation. More specifically in *sitār* it refers to fast oscillation between notes by pulling the string.

Gat   Fixed composition with *tāl* in instrumental music.

Gayaki   In instrumental music it is a way of playing using the inflections and general style of vocal music.

Gharānā   Literally, household. Guild-like organisations of musicians representing a particular style of playing or singing.

Ghasīt   A slide between two notes.

Guru   Teacher or master.

Jawal-sawab   Question–answer interplay between two instruments.

Jhāllā   Section of a *rāg* in instrumental music concentrating on fast rhythmic variations.

Joṛ   Section of a *rāg* in instrumental music, between the *ālāp* and the *gat*.

Khyāl   Genre of North Indian classical vocal music.

Krintan   Type of ornamentation in instrumental music.

Laya   Tempo and rhythmic flow.

Layakārī   Playing with the rhythm or tempo of the music.

Madhya   Medium or middle. Can refer to tempo or octave.

Masītkhanī   Particular kind of *sitār* composition with special *bol* pattern.

Mātrā   Beat.

Mīnd   The smooth passage between notes, e.g. on the *sitār* by lateral deflection of the string.

Mohṛā   A punctuation point in the *ālāp* section of a performance where the music picks up a definite pulse for a few beats.

Mukhra   The opening phrase of a composition in vocal or instrumental music.

Palṭā   Practice pattern using various permutations of notes.

Qawwalī   Muslim devotional song.

Quāidā   Literally, formula. Stroke pattern used as basis for improvisation in *tablā* playing.

Rāg   The organisation of melodic material in Indian music. Each *rāg* is related back to a parent scale (*thāt*) and has particular ascending and descending patterns of notes, identifying phrases, altered notes, and so on. The aesthetic dimension of *rāgs* also assigns them to particular times of the day and seasons of the year.

Razakhanī   A type of composition in *sitār* playing.

Saptak   An octave.

Sargam   Syllabic names for the seven pitches in Indian music: SA, RE, GA, MA, PA, DHA, NI, SA.

RE, GA, DHA and NI can be flattened (*komal*). MA can be sharpened (*tivra*). SA and PA are fixed. Notes in their natural position are called *shuddha*. *Komal* notes are indicated: R̲E̲, G̲A̲, etc. *Tivra* MA: MÁ. Dots above or below indicate the octave.

Shishya   Pupil, disciple.

Sitār   North Indian plucked lute-type instrument.

Sthāyī   Section of a composition, usually in the middle octave.

Sum   First beat of a rhythmic cycle.

Svara   A note or degree of scale.

Tablā   North Indian pair of drums. Used as solo as well as accompanying instrument.

Tāl   Metric system of Indian classical music. A rhythmic cycle made up of recurring groupings of beats, for example *tīntāl*:

Tīntāl (16 beats)

X	2	0	3	X
1 2 3 4	5 6 7 8	9 10 11 12	13 14 15 16	1 etc.

The group of beats from 9–12 is known as *khālī* (empty). The first beat is called *sum*.

Tīntāl is the most common *tāl* in Indian classical music, but there are many others with various numbers of beats: 10, 14, 7, 6, 8, etc.

Tānpūrā   A fretless North Indian plucked lute with four to six strings, used as a drone accompaniment in both vocal and instrumental music.

Tār   Highest octave.

Taraf   Name of sympathetic strings on instruments.

Thāt   Scale-type.

Ṭhekā   Stroke pattern for keeping *tāl* on *tablā*.

Ṭhumṛi   Genre of classical vocal music.

Tihāī   Literally, third. A thrice-played rhythmic cadence used to punctuate sections of improvisation.

Tīntāl   See above under *tāl*.

Vikrit   Literally, crooked. Patterns of notes that are not straight in ascent or descent.

Vilambit   Slow.

Vistar   Slow improvisation, particularly in vocal music. Can also be played in this style in instrumental music.

Yaman   The name of a popular *rāg* which uses a sharpened 4th note.

Bibliography

Chaudhuri, Debu
1981   *Sitar and its technique*   Delhi: Avon Book Co.
Good *sitār* teaching manual with compositions in all the major *rāgs*.

Danielou, A.
1980   *The rāgs of Northern Indian music*   New Delhi: Munshiram Manoharlal
A detailed collection of *rāgs* showing their structure and examining their historical/philosophical background. Also includes valuable information on *tāl*.

1984   *Grove's Dictionary of Musical Instruments,* 3 vols   London: Macmillan
Excellent articles on Indian musical instruments and their repertoire by Alistair Dick and others.

Jairazbhoy, N.
1971   *The rāgs of North Indian music*   London: Faber & Faber
Complex and detailed study of the evolution of North Indian *rāgs* and their structures. Includes recorded examples of *sitār*.

Neuman, D.
1980   *The life of music in North India*   New Delhi: Manohar
Fascinating study of the social context of contemporary Indian classical music, giving interesting insights into the reality of musicians' lives.

Kaufmann, W.
1984   *The ragas of North India*   New York: Da Capo Press
A huge 'dictionary' of *rāgs* with specimen compositions and general information on aesthetic and historical background. Invaluable as a reference book. There is also a second volume which deals with the *rāgs* of South India.

Sorrell, N. & Narayan, R.
1980   *Indian music in performance: a practical introduction*   Manchester University Press
Goes through a typical performance in detail, with cassette. A wealth of useful information on practice, improvisation, melodic details of *rāgs*, and a section on instruments. Gives interesting background and history of the *sārangī*.

Shankar, R.
n.d.   *Learning Indian music – a systematic approach* (book with three cassettes)   Lauderdale: Onomatopoeia Inc.
Excellent teaching material. Goes through *rāg* and *tāl* in detail with exercises and examples on tape putting the material into a performance context.

Shankar, R.
1969   *My music, my life*   London: Jonathan Cape
Interesting background to the life and music of Ravi Shankar. Also has information on theory and instruments. Contains *sitār* teaching material.

Wade, B.
1979   *Music in India: the classical traditions*   New Jersey: Prentice Hall
Comprehensive introduction to both North and South Indian music with useful discography, bibliography, etc.

Some of the above books may be difficult to buy, being (probably) out of print, but most can be found in any good library, along with many other titles related to Indian music.

Discography

The availability of specific recordings is highly unpredictable, so some of the principal artists are listed here.

Vocal music

Khyāl and Ṭhumṛi Ustad Bade Ghulam Ali, Bhimsen Joshi, Ustad Amir Khan, Lakshmi Shankar, Nirmala Devi.

Dhrupad N. M. Dagar and N. A. Dagar.

Instrumental music

Sitār Ravi Shankar, Ustad Vilayat Khan, Ustad Imrat Khan, Nikhil Banerjee, Budhaditya Mukherjee, Debu Chaudhuri, Halim Jaffar Khan.

Sarod Ustad Ali Akbar Khan, Ustad Amjad Ali Khan, Sharan Rani.

Sāraṅgī Ram Narayan.

Shehnai Ustad Bismillah Khan.

Bansurī Pannalal Ghosh, Hariprasad Chaurasia.

Tablā Latif Ahmed Khan, Alla Rakha, Shanta Prasad, Zakir Hussein, Shafaat Ahmed Khan, Kishan Maharaj, Anindo Chatterjee, Swapan Chaudhuri, Sharda Sahai.

These are some suggestions, but obviously there are many more fine artists who can be heard on record.

Contents of cassette

The cassette (ISBN 0 521 38411 7) that accompanies this book contains the following items.

Side A

Music example

Assignment 11	16	*Tāns* in *rāg* Yaman (*sitār* and *tablā*)
		a. 4-beat *tān*
		8-beat *tān*
		12-beat *tān*
		16-beat *tān*
		b. the same *tāns* without a break
Assignment 12	17	*Quāidā* in *tīntāl* (*tablā* and voice)
	18	Improvisation on *quāidā* (*tablā* and voice)

Side B

A performance of *rāg Yaman*:
– *ālāp*
– *joṛ*
– *gat* in *tīntāl* (16 beats)
– *jhāllā*

Performers: Gerry Farrell – *sitār*
            Jaspal Bhogal – *tablā*